Contents

THE MARK of a CHRISTIAN

THE MARK of a CHRISTIAN

Studies From 2 Corinthians

JAMES THOMPSON

RESOURCE □ PUBLICATIONS

202 S. Locust
Searcy, AR 72143

Preface

The power of Scripture, I believe, is to be found in the capacity of ancient documents to address the questions of our own time. When this book was originally written in 1983, churches were asking new questions because of the changed situation in our culture. What kind of church do we want to be? What form and style of leadership reflects who we are as a people? A consumer-oriented culture was tempting the church to measure its own success by the standards of the marketplace. A culture influenced by a consumer mentality was challenging the church's understanding of itself.

As we move toward the end of a millennium, those questions have become even more urgent. Churches are increasingly confronted by the demands of members who come as consumers, and who are engaged in comparative shopping in search of the most benefits.

The epistle of 2 Corinthians offers a powerful message for our own time, for here Paul was faced with a Christian community in the process of determining what kind of church it would be. The Pauline mission, measured by the standards of the ancient culture, was a failure, and Paul was a failure as a minister. Paul's task was to introduce a young church to the "new world" (2 Corinthians 5:17) that is measured by the cross, and not human standards.

Our situation is not unlike that of the Corinthians. This ancient church was confused by the competing claims of ministers who appeared to be more successful than Paul. Against their claims, Paul offered a ministry that was shaped by the cross of Christ. This book is written in the hope that we will overhear the conversation between Paul and the Corinthians, and that we will resist the temptation to measure our effectiveness by the standards of our culture. I wish to express my gratitude to Eddie Cloer and Resource Publications for the republication of *The Mark of a Christian*.

James Thompson

1

THE MARK OF A CHRISTIAN
(10:1-10)

"... as he is Christ's, so are we" (10:7).

A well-known minister has told a parable about a lifesaving station that was established on a dangerous seacoast where ships were frequently wrecked. Its volunteers repeatedly risked their lives while rescuing men from drowning. As the lifesaving station grew, the members put up sheds for the boats and for the shelter of those who were pulled from the sea. Then they erected a building where the shipwreck victims could be comfortable. The members took great pleasure in the building, especially after they had added a restaurant, game rooms, and a lounge for themselves. The station then grew in prestige and more influential members joined them. After a while, the members then hired workers to do the lifesaving for them while they enjoyed the club.

This development disturbed some of the members of the lifesaving station so much that they decided that the purpose of the original station had been lost. Consequently, they resigned and started a lifesaving station farther down the coast. As the years passed, the new station went through the same development as the original station until another group pulled away and started their own station. If you visit that seacoast today, you will find a whole series of exclusive clubs on the shore. Not one of them, however, is much interested in lifesaving, though many shipwrecks still take place in those waters.

The meaning of the story is not difficult to find. We are aware that institutions easily lose touch with their original purpose, even while they show signs of vitality and strength. This process also happens in the life and ministry of the church. Today, there is an extraordinary variety of programs in local congregations, indicating considerable strength and vitality. When we observe the many alternative models of life, certain important questions must be asked. Are all of the alternative models equally authentic for the purpose of the church? What standards may we use in determining which programs are authentic? Is it possible that the church can become, like the lifesaving station, far removed from its original purpose?

The usual portrayal of Christianity in the media suggests that widespread cynicism about religious institutions. The minister is commonly depicted as hypocritical and self-serving. Sinclair Lewis' Elmer Gantry was a huckster who used religion to enrich himself and manipulate the masses. The media often appear to delight in stories which indicate that religious people and institutions are nothing more than agents for enriching themselves. In one of the greatest masterpieces of literature, Dostoevski told a story in which serious doubts were raised about the authenticity of organized religion. In the story of the Grand Inquisitor (*The Brothers Karamazov*), Jesus Christ returns to the earth in a little Spanish town. He is quickly placed in jail by the forces of organized religion, who tell him that he has no right to interfere with their operation. Finally, Jesus is told, "Go, and come no more. Come not at all—never, never!" The author's point was that Christianity can lose its authenticity.

Those who question the authenticity of Christianity are usually not nearly so interested in asking whether Christians represent true Christian doctrine as they are in asking about the genuineness of the Christians themselves. The common criticism, as in *Elmer Gantry*, is that Christian leaders are hucksters and that churches are interested in nothing other than the extension of their power and influence. While Christians may give lofty claims about being different from the standards of the rest of the world, they are criticized because they have chosen the world's standards over those of Jesus Christ.

We might at first not be concerned about the common portrayals of churches and ministers, for we might conclude that this "credibility gap" is someone else's problem. We might also conclude that those who wish to portray Christian leaders as opportunists are biased in their appraisal. But I am convinced that we cannot dismiss these questions easily, for it is possible for us to fail to meet the test of authenticity. Indeed, we can say the right things and go through the right motions and still not be authentic Christians.

The question of authenticity is fundamental to our existence as a church because it confronts us in different ways. There is a place, for example, for a congregation to ask periodically about the "state of the church" and to determine what programs are necessary for an authentic church. Our budgets and our buildings will reflect our view of authenticity. Our selection of ministers and other leaders will also reflect our understanding of authentic Christianity. We will select leaders who are, in our judgment, authentic Christians. Indeed, almost every decision we make will be based on the prior question: What is the distinguishing mark of the Christian?

Behind the realities of budgets and buildings is the more fundamental question: What is the mark of an authentic church? In our society, we do not lack answers. The problem is that we are often overwhelmed by contradictory answers. Authentic Christianity has come to mean different things to different people. A lack of agreement over this question can have disastrous results within a local congregation. Some may contend that the mark of an authentic Christian is a personal religious experience. This response is heard among those who point to feelings and signs which demonstrate the genuineness of their ministry. A second answer has been the test of visible success. In a culture where visible results are greatly admired, we can easily apply that test to our own Christianity. We are tempted to apply the standard of the marketplace to our Christian faith. When this standard is applied, the mark of authenticity is reduced to a set of numbers on a page. One can determine the success or failure of a church by reading the figures which register net gains and losses in membership and net assets. If this standard is applied, the church leaders have the responsibility of improving the church's image in order to make it as attractive to as many people as possible.

In other instances, the test of authenticity has been limited to questions about the church's involvement in relieving social and economic oppression. Others have said that the test is to be seen primarily in certain doctrines and themes which hold an important place in the church. Therefore, many different versions of the mark of the Christian are heard.

This question has especially concerned ministers whose task is to equip a congregation for ministry. Because of the many contradictory views of ministry, those who are involved in full-time work are apt to suffer from an identity crisis in discovering appropriate models for their work. In many instances, the minister's model for his activity has been derived from outside the church. Some have expected the minister to measure up to the standards of the corporation in maximizing efficiency and growth. Others have seen his model in the professional counselor. This "identity crisis" is the problem, not only of the minister, but of the whole church. We have seen so many alternative versions that we must return to ask the fundamental question: What is the mark of a Christian?

OVERHEARING THE NEW TESTAMENT (10:1-10)

One reason for the continuing power of the New Testament is that our questions were already being asked in the first century. Indeed, it was because of questions like our own that the Epistles were written. If we are intent on discovering what authentic ministry is, we will benefit from "overhearing" the discussion which took place between Paul and the Corinthians. Beginning with the founding of the Corinthian church (cf. Acts 18:1-17), Paul had a stormy relationship with a congregation which seemed to go from one crisis to another. These crises were not even settled with the writing of 1 Corinthians. As soon as Paul wrote 1 Corinthians, a whole new set of problems arose. Apparently, Timothy, who had delivered 1 Corinthians, returned to Paul to tell him that there were new questions.

The new issues facing the Corinthians are stated in 10:1-11. We notice immediately that Paul writes as a man under attack. Indeed, 10:1, 2 shows that Paul has been criticized. We probably notice a bit of sarcasm in 10:1, for Paul is probably referring to the common criticisms that were lodged against him. According to 10:2, "some" are saying that Paul has been "acting in a worldly fashion" (*kata sarka*, "according to the flesh"). The issue is stated more forcefully in 10:7, where Paul says, ". . . If any one is confident that he is Christ's, let him remind himself that he is Christ's, so are we." The word "Christ's" (literally, "of Christ") could be rendered, "Christian." The issue at stake in 2 Corinthians is this: What is the mark of a Christian? Paul is a man under attack who is having to give his credentials as a Christian. This is the central issue of 2 Corinthians.

Paul appears to be on the defensive throughout 2 Corinthians. These who question his Christian ministry apparently arrived in Corinth after the writing of 1 Corinthians. They came with their own letters of recommendation (3:1), and they claimed to be "servants of Christ" (11:5; 12:11). At the same time, they compare themselves to Paul, concluding that he is not a true "servant of Christ" (11:23). There are indications throughout the book that they delight in comparing themselves to other ministers and in measuring their powers with those of other ministers (cf. 3:1; 10:12, 18). Paul is in an awkward position, therefore. It is not his choice to "class or compare himself" (10:12) with other ministers. Yet, for the sake of the church he must declare that he is an authentic Christian. His claim in 10:7 is similar to his affirmation in 11:23, "Are they servants of Christ? . . . I more so. . . ."

Paul's claim that he is a "true Christian" is a reminder to us that often the major issue is the behavior and lifestyle of the servant, and not a specific doctrine. His opponents have not questioned his convictions; they have questioned his actions as a minister of Christ. Indeed, a brief look at a concordance illustrates how important the theme of ministry is in 2 Corinthians. The words "minister" (*diakonos*) and "ministry" (*diakonia*) appear almost as frequently in 2 Corinthians as in the rest of Paul's letters combined, although the English translations often use other words. *Diakonia* is employed eleven times (cf. 3:7-9; 4:1; 5:18; 6:3; 8:4; 11:8), while *diakonos* is employed four times (3:6; 6:4; 11:5, 23). The frequent use of this word suggests that authentic ministry is the theme of 2 Corinthians. Paul writes the letter in order to defend his ministry from attack.

THE MARK OF A CHRISTIAN

What is the mark of a legitimate servant of Christ? On what basis do we claim, with Paul, that we are "Christ's" (10:7)? From the charges that were made against Paul in 10:1-11, we can recognize the "test" which Paul's critics imposed: "For they say, 'His letters are weighty and strong, but his bodily presence is weak, and his speech of no account' " (10:10). Paul was not an impressive spokesman. Indeed, the criticism was, expressed literally, "His speech arouses contempt." As one who was in constant ill health (12:7), his "bodily presence" was weak. His "humility" (10:1) gave the impression that he had no courage and "presence" in his work. These criticisms added up to the charge that Paul acted "in a worldly way" (literally, "according to the flesh"). The opponents appeared to be saying, "If Paul were really a Christian, there would be some sign of power, some manifestation of persuasive oratory or a success record." Paul's unimpressive showing suggested that he was neither a Christian (10:7) nor a servant of Christ (1:23).

The "mark" of the Christian, said the opponents, must come in visible manifestations of power. An unimpressive showing is for them a sign that he is lacking the power of the Spirit. When they accuse Paul of conducting his ministry in a "worldly fashion," they are actually accusing him of lacking the Spirit. The term "worldly fashion" (*kata sarka*) is normally the opposite of "according to the Spirit" (*kata pneuma*, Romans 8:4, 5). Paul, with his "weak" physical presence and speech, has failed to pass their test of authenticity.

We can feel some of Paul's sarcasm when he responds to their charges: "I, Paul, myself entreat you, by the meekness and gentleness of Christ—I who am humble when face to face with you, but bold to you when I am away!" (10:1).

"Meekness and gentleness" are not, for Paul, shameful. By the worldly standards, "meekness and gentleness" were contemptible. The terms suggested a cringing and humiliating stance. But the characteristics which the world considered weak were for Paul the mark of a Christian, a proper demeanor for serving Christ. The characteristics which disqualified him in the eyes of his opponents were accepted by him as a sign that he was Christ's (10:7). He appeals to his readers by the "meekness and gentleness of Christ." Christ was Himself the model for Paul's ministry.

A CHURCH CAUGHT IN THE MIDDLE

We can sympathize with the Corinthians as they listened to Paul and his opponents commend themselves (5:12; 6:4) as authentic Christians. Each side claimed to offer the credentials of legitimate servants of Christ while offering different standards of measurement. The church was called upon to decide what kind of church it was to be by choosing the one ministry which was authentic. We assume that the Corinthians made the right decision, inasmuch as they preserved Paul's words and not those of his opponents.

The situation of the original readers was not very different from that of every congregation today. We see possibilities for programs today which we never considered a few years ago. We stand before alternatives which force us to decide what kind of church we want to be. Because of these opportunities, there is a good reason for us to see that we share the same questions which lie behind 2 Corinthians. The credentials of the authentic Christian that are mentioned in 2 Corinthians are also the signs of the servant of Christ today. Paul challenges the very ones who were examining him: "Examine yourselves, to see whether you are holding to your faith" (13:5).

ON READING 2 CORINTHIANS

The reader of 2 Corinthians can hardly fail to recognize that, while practically every page of the book concerns the subject of authentic Christianity. Paul's tone and focus seem to shift radically at times. Some sections of the letter suggest that Paul was elated that Titus has brought the good news that the Corinthians have repented from their previous challenge to Paul's work. In these sections, we have the impression that Paul's mind, which had been tormented by the Corinthians' problems (2:12, 13), is now at rest. However, in chapters 10 through 13, Paul's tone suggests that his ministry is under serious attack. He is forced to demonstrate to the church which he founded that he is a true Christian (10:7; 11:23)! Preparing for a third visit to the church, he is uncertain what kind of reception he will find there. He fears that he will face problems similar to those that he had faced on his second trip to Corinth (cf. 2:1-4). These chapters indicate dramatically that the problems are not over. Church life remains stormy!

Other sections of 2 Corinthians seem to interrupt the flow of the discussion. For example, 6:14—7:1, a section warning Christians against being "bound together with unbelievers," seems to interrupt the thoughts of 6:13 and 7:2. In addition, the book seems to have two separate lessons on the need for participating in the collection (chapters 8 and 9). The second lesson begins in 9:1: "Now it is superfluous for me to write to you about the offering for the saints. . . ."

There is no easy explanation for the apparent interruptions in the flow of this epistle. Scholars have debated why, in the same book, the problems sometime seem to be settled (chapter 7) and at other times to be far from being settled (chapters 10 through 13). These interruptions suggest that the letter was not written at one sitting. Perhaps the situation in Corinth changed several times. Paul's changing mood may reflect the changing situation in that church. These changes within the epistle can remind us that church life for us is not unlike the experience of the Corinthian church. Scarcely is there a time when all the problems have been settled, but those are often nothing more than passing moments in the history of the church. The letters to the Corinthians remind us that church life has always been filled with moments of tension.

CONCLUSION

What is the mark of the true Christian? What programs of the church carry on the work of the one who "came not to be served, but to serve"? The Corinthians were faced with that decision. The contemporary church, faced with various options in planning its programs, is faced with the same kind of decision. For that reason, 2 Corinthians answers the questions which we are asking.

2

PROMISES TO KEEP
(1:12—2:4)

"... to let you know the abundant love
I have for you" (2:4).

The scandals involving a number of institutions in recent years have undoubtedly contributed to a cynicism about all institutions and their leaders among a wide segment of the population. The term "public servant" has taken an ironic meaning after the sensational news stories of those who did not serve the public at all. The scandals do not suggest that all public and private institutions are directed by self-serving, corrupt leaders whose one purpose is to advance themselves and defraud the public. Unfortunately, though, they have been the cause of doubt and cynicism, making it necessary for every institution to demonstrate its legitimacy to the public.

A widespread cynicism naturally becomes a factor in church life. We do not only face the doctrinal issues which are meant to determine what authentic ministry is. Nor are we only concerned to find the correct model for ministry. There is the necessity of demonstrating the integrity of those participating in the various ministries of the church. The cynicism of the day has given us the eyes and ears to examine every decision and program of the church for signs of self-promotion.

The common criticism is that those who claim to speak for God and be "new creatures" (5:17) are not different from anyone else: Important decisions about the Christian life and about one's place of service are made on the basis of calculated and worldly standards. Some Christians locate a place to serve in the same way that they take a position with a company: by asking which group will be best for *their* achievement. We choose church leaders by the same standards employed by the rest of the world. According to the cynic's view, the minister is for sale, always prepared to turn from one ministry to another if the move will lead to his advancement and recognition.

The cynic is, obviously, not always correct. We do not always use worldly standards in making our decisions. But we are frequently tempted to use the worldly criteria for establishing the mission of the church and our own place within it. The "me generation" in which we live offers the temptation for us to look first to our own advancement. Undoubtedly, the cynic has been right some of the time.

Second Corinthians is a reaction to the kinds of criticism that are commonly offered today. It seems outrageous that Paul should be placed on the defensive by the very church which he had founded, and that he should need to answer their charges and give proof (13:3) that Christ speaks in him. The remarkable fact about the book is that he carefully responds to the charges because it is not enough only to act with integrity; others need to know that we have acted with integrity (cf. 1:13, 14; 13:6).

THE ISSUE IS THE MESSENGER

Paul's common practice in writing his letters was to indicate very early the dominant concern which evoked the writing of the letter. His letters were always written in response to concrete problems. Usually, this dominant concern was stated immediately after the thanksgiving (or blessing) section. In 2 Corinthians, this dominant concern is in 1:12-14, which sets the tone of the epistle. The issue of 2 Corinthians, as these verses show, is the behavior of the apostle. Paul writes 2 Corinthians to defend how "we have behaved in the world" (1:12). The tone suggests that his personal demeanor is under attack. He wants his readers to "understand fully" (1:13).

"There is one thing we are proud of," says Paul (1:12; NEB). Paul's word for "proud" (*kauchesis*) normally appears with the negative connotation, "boast." The word normally conveys the idea of one who boasts about his work (cf. Romans 3:27; 4:2) apart from God's role. In 2 Corinthians, this word has a special meaning, for the opponents of Paul have boasted of their own deeds, suggesting that he is a poor apostle by comparison (cf. 5:12; 10:13, 17). Their boasting has been based on human standards.

There is, however, an appropriate kind of boasting (cf. 1 Corinthians 1:31) which is "of the Lord" and acknowledges its indebtedness before God. The words for "boast" (*kauchesis, kauchema*) are used for "being proud of" one's work. Paul says in Romans, "In Christ Jesus, then, I have reason to be proud of my work for God" (Romans 15:17). In 2 Corinthians, he frequently responds to the boasting of others by recalling those actions in which he "takes pride" (1:16; 12:1, 9). According to Paul, one may "be proud of" others. According to 7:4, he has "great pride" in the church which he founded (cf. 9:2). Indeed, Paul states what he is "proud of" in 1:12 in order that his readers can be "proud of" him. This fact suggests that the true servant of Christ can take pride in a style of behavior that is distinctively Christian. A great portion of 2 Corinthians is composed of Paul's reminders of specific details of his ministry which "commend" him (6:4) as a legitimate servant of Christ.

Second Corinthians is characterized by an extraordinary amount of autobiographical detail from Paul, and most of it is a form of boasting which was done in self-defense (cf. 6:1-10; 11:23-33). Our natural response is to be uncomfortable with any kind of boasting. Paul's experience suggests that there is a place for recalling the details which establish our credibility. We are reticent to speak in such personal terms of our own experiences and to listen to others who recall their own history. But Paul's "boast" is a reminder that sometimes we need to demonstrate that we have not become slothful and unconcerned about our ministry. It is in concrete deeds that we show that we "take pride" in our work.

Paul has to answer the same charge that the Christian today

commonly must answer: that "worldly" considerations determine his behavior. He denies that he acted with "earthly wisdom [*en sophia sarkike*]" (1:12). ". . . Do I make my plans like a worldly man [*kata sarka*]?" he asks (1:17). Behind this defense is the charge that he speaks and acts "from a human point of view [*kata sarka*]" (5:16), not like a "new creation" (5:17) who lives by the gift of the Spirit. That is, some are saying that the flesh (*sarx* in 1:12, 17; 5:16) governs Paul's life. His opponents claim that he is no different from anyone else, and that he is as calculating and self-serving as anyone.

Against that background, Paul claims that he did behave as a spiritual man, and that he behaved with "holiness and godly sincerity." This issue was apparently important, for Paul insists in 2:17 that he has conducted his life with sincerity. Paul has not escaped the charge that he is "crafty" or "tricky," in his ministry. Thus he claims that Christ has made a difference in his behavior (1:12-14).

Paul's defense reminds us that no one escapes the close scrutiny of the cynic. At times, church leaders and those who are engaged in various ministries will be observed for signs that they are not Christian in their behavior. The price we pay in making the claim that we are a "new creation" is that we are challenged to demonstrate that something is "new" in the work to which we have committed ourselves.

CHRISTIANS AND THEIR DECISIONS

The incident that led to doubts about Paul's sincerity was like situations which often occur among us that lead to misunderstandings. Paul had once promised the Corinthians that he would spend an extended period with them, perhaps even the winter (1 Corinthians 16:5, 6), on his trip to Macedonia (1:15, 16). According to 1:25, Paul's plans did not work out. This change of plans led to the charge that he was "fickle" and "worldly" in his decision-making. We can imagine the misunderstandings that could grow out of such an incident: "He does not keep his commitments"; "You cannot trust him because his word is no good. He will change plans without notice if it is to his advantage." These are serious charges against one of Christ's servants.

No one can serve Christ successfully when his loyalty and faithfulness are in doubt. Consequently, Paul shows in 1:18-20 that his word has been reliable. ". . . our word to you has not been Yes and No" (1:18). Then he recalls that the Christian proclamation has never been an unclear "Yes and No." In every worship service, when the church says, "Amen," it recalls that Jesus is God's "Yes." Indeed, Paul sums up all of Scripture under the heading of God's promise. The church knows in Jesus that God's Word "shall not return to me empty" and that "it shall accomplish that which I purpose" (Isaiah 55:11).

The little essay on God's faithfulness to His Word (1:30) seems, at first glance, out of place in Paul's defense of his behavior. But it is vitally important for Paul to demonstrate that his behavior is consistent with the God who keeps His word. There is a connection between God's nature and the character of the authentic minister.

What is the mark of the Christian? One test, according to Paul, is the reliability of one's word and the keeping of commitments to others. The true servant of Christ does not only announce God's faithfulness to His Word in Jesus Christ. The mark of a Christian is that he also embodies a lifestyle to others.

This test of authenticity is unlikely to be appreciated in our culture, for the keeping of commitments is a low priority item. The propaganda of our age tells us to "keep our options open" and to be infinitely adaptable. "Keeping our options open" thus involves the refusal to make commitments that are not to our personal advantage. The propaganda of our age suggests that it is even impossible to commit oneself indefinitely to a spouse, for such a commitment interferes with personal freedom. We are a culture which insists on standing at the sidelines, always prepared to follow the option that enriches ourselves.

This "worldly" view has an obvious temptation for the church. It is hard to remain loyal to a church that has problems. Those who choose to share the pain of commitment pay a high psychological and physical cost in remaining faithful to a community whose problems are beyond their control. For example, the changing character of the neighborhood or city certainly leaves the church vulnerable. A church may suffer because of the wrong decisions which were made in the past. We may find ourselves even dissatisfied with a recurring pattern of decisions which seem to display weak leadership. From a "human point of view," the appropriate response is to "keep our options open" and resist becoming involved with the problems of a community.

Paul insists, when others accuse him of being fickle, that his behavior is consistent with the gospel. From the God who says "Yes" to His promises, he has learned to take his personal commitments seriously. Even if circumstances demanded a change in his plans, his moves were not dictated by personal expediency. For Paul, there was a personal character which was formed by the gospel story.

Paul's defense indicates that authentic discipleship is not only a matter of saying the right things. It involves also a behavior that is consistent with our message. Sören Kierkegaard tells about a man who escaped from the insane asylum only to face the real prospect of being recognized as insane by the people in the next town and being returned to the institution. He decided to disguise his insanity by uttering aloud some generally accepted truth that would prove to all who heard him that he was sane. He walked down the street, saying to each passerby, "The earth is round. The earth is round." Needless to say, he was recognized and returned to the insane asylum. The narrator of this story was suggesting that it is not enough to tell the truth. There is something nonsensical about the truth in the mouth of one whose life has not been affected by that truth.[1]

The true Christian has been formed by the story. While it is true that we preach Christ and not ourselves, there is an "I" in our proclamation and teaching. The recurrence in 2 Corinthians of the "I" is a reminder that the gospel is convincing only if

---

[1] Sören Kierkegaard, *Concluding Unscientific Postscript,* trans. David Swenson and Walter Lowrie (Princeton: Princeton University Press, 1941), 159; quoted in Fred Craddock, *Overhearing the Gospel* (Nashville, Tenn.: Abingdon Press, 1978), 50.

its servant is convincing.

Against the charge that Paul is a "worldly" (literally, "man of the flesh," 1:12) man, Paul reminds his readers that the God who keeps His Word has both commissioned him (1:21) and given the Spirit to the church as a "guarantee" (1:22; cf. 5:5; Ephesians 1:14). God's guarantee, already present in the church through the Spirit, is a reminder of His reliability. Paul behaves in a way that is consistent with the faithfulness of God.

"THE ABUNDANT LOVE I HAVE FOR YOU"

Why did Paul not keep his word and thus open up his motives to scrutiny? He gives a clear answer in 1:23 when he says, ". . . it was to spare you that I refrained from coming to Corinth." He then describes a stormy relationship with the Corinthian church, which has been recorded nowhere else. As 1:3—2:13 demonstrates, the Corinthian church has caused Paul much grief. On one occasion Paul made a painful visit (2:1) to deal with an open rebellion by someone who had caused great pain (2:5). He later wrote a letter "out of much affliction and anguish of heart" (2:4). On a later occasion, Paul went to Troas, where he had hoped to meet Titus. Even in the midst of a successful missionary labor ("a door was opened for me in the Lord"), Paul took "leave" and went on to Macedonia (2:13). The extent of Paul's concern is stated in 2:13, where he says, "But my mind could not rest because I did not find my brother Titus there. . . ." He risked a successful mission for the sake of a disobedient church!

From a human point of view, Paul's values seem strangely out of place in remaining emotionally involved with a troublesome church. We do not easily understand his willingness to give up a possibility for great success in order to deal with a contentious and ungrateful church. But Paul was moved, as he says later (11:28), by the "daily pressure upon me of my anxiety for all the churches." We might say, in contemporary language, that the mark of the Christian for Paul is the acceptance of stress for the sake of the church.

Paul's "anxiety for all the churches" and his constant pressure indicate a selflessness which runs counter to "the human point of view." His actions demonstrate that he acted only out of concern for others. "It was to spare you. . . ." he says (1:23). Remarkably, he says that he acted in order to show the "abundant love" (2:4) he had for this disobedient church. This particular church was not easy to love.

We speak often of the need to avoid situations of stress. Some say that ministers and others should not take the problems of the church home with them. But the mark of the Christian is the readiness to suffer inconvenience for the sake of others. It may include telephone calls at inconvenient times and meetings which interfere with our normal plans. It involves the will to empty ourselves for others. The model for our work is not the manager who can place a "Do not disturb!" sign on his door whenever he desires; it is the "man for others" who gave His life for many.

Paul's model was the One who gave Himself for others. By suffering grief with the church, he demonstrated the impact of the cross on his life. "One died for all; therefore all died" (5:14). This fact meant the end of living for oneself (5:15).

CONCLUSION

What is the mark of the Christian? For Paul, it is a life which shows that he has been shaped by the story. "Look at the record," he seems to be saying, "and see if it is the record of a huckster." "Look at my personal story, and see if it conforms to *the story*." This response is the ultimate mark of the Christian.

We, in our own ministries, are compiling a record to which we must refer, for this record is the testimony to our commitment. If the issue is the messenger as well as the message, the messenger's conduct will show whether he has been shaped by the message he proclaims.

3

PRISONERS FOR GOD
(2:14-17)

"We are not . . . peddlers of God's Word; . . ." (2:17).

Years ago I stood with thousands of people on a cold November day to watch and listen as a candidate for President of the United States made a last-minute appeal to both supporters and the uncommitted to support his candidacy. While I remember little of what was said, I remember distinctly the atmosphere which the event was intended to create. Everything had been carefully managed to look "upbeat." Both the supporters and the uncommitted were to believe that victory was in sight. The planners knew that millions throughout the country would see a one-minute segment of the event on television that evening. The one message which they wished to communicate was that this cause could win. They knew that no one wanted to involve himself in a lost cause.

As these professionals knew, a "bandwagon" mentality leads us to associate ourselves with a winner. Often we must be convinced that worthy causes have within them the signs of success before we risk ourselves on their behalf. Lost causes simply have no appeal to us.

We naturally wish to see the sign of triumph in the church. The anticipation of victory is infectious, stimulating both the dedicated Christians and those who are uncommitted. Consequently, we attempt to create a positive atmosphere. We like to point to the growth in everything that is measurable to show that victory is near. We compare this year's attendance with last year's. We point to increases in giving, new statistics in conversion, and increases in the church's property. These signs of victory are used to show that our program is no lost cause and to stimulate us to look for other signs of victory.

As verse 14 shows, it is natural to rejoice in victory: "But thanks be to God, who in Christ always leads us in triumph, . . ." Paul shares our delight at the thrill of victory. At times, the only suitable words for our experience are Paul's words: "Thanks be to God" (cf. Romans 6:17; 7:25). The simple exclamation suggests a sense of awe at what God has done in Jesus Christ. The New Testament leaves no doubt that authentic Christianity includes this sense of wonder when only exclamations are adequate. It was for this reason that early Christians were often moved to break out in singing. They shared Paul's sense of wonder as he said, "But thanks be to God, who in Christ always leads us in triumph, . . ." (2:14).

TRIUMPHANT CHRISTIANITY

Paul uses a colorful image for the victory of Christianity: ". . . who in Christ always leads us in triumph, . . ." The image was derived from the triumphal processionals of ancient Rome. Triumphant generals returned home from battle before adoring crowds, exhibiting the signs of victory. These tokens of victory included the captives and the booty brought home from war. Thus, Paul declares with an exclamation that God's cause has its own triumphant processional. Just as the general marched through the city in triumph, God leads His people in triumph.

The note of triumph is common in the New Testament. The word translated "leads us in triumph" in verse 14 (*thriambeuo*) is used also in Colossians 2:15 for the victory achieved by Christ at the cross when he says, "He disarmed the principalities and powers and made a public example of them, *triumphing over them* in him." It is as if we were fighting a battle with the assurance that victory is already determined.

Paul's epistles abound in reference to the victory which Christ has won. The conclusion which he draws from the resurrection of Christ is, "But thanks be to God, who gives us the victory through our Lord Jesus Christ" (1 Corinthians 15:57). The promise of victory leads him to announce the victory of Christ in beautiful, lyrical terms in Romans 8:37: "No, in all these things we are more than conquerors through him who loved us." It was triumphant Christianity, therefore, that led Paul to exclaim on more than one occasion, "Thanks be to God!"

Our ministries demand that we share with Paul this certainty of God's ultimate victory. Despair can be as infectious as hope. It can rob us of the will to serve and communicate hopelessness to others, producing its own kind of perverse "bandwagon" effect. The mark of the Christian is the participation in a victory processional.

WHAT KIND OF TRIUMPH?

Anyone who reads 2 Corinthians from the beginning to Paul's remarkable exclamation in 2:14 is sure to be amazed at the abruptness of Paul's claim of victory. In the immediate context of the passage, Paul has been on the defensive. He has answered various charges that he is insincere and fickle. In 2:1-13, he has been recalling the intense grief which has accompanied his ministry with the Corinthians. He has written a letter to the Corinthians "out of much affliction and anguish of heart and with many tears" (2:4). Both he and his readers have experienced pain (2:2, 5). He tells of when his mind "could not rest" because of his concern with the Corinthian church and its problems and his failure to meet Titus and receive the news about them. The remarkable fact about the victory claim in verse 14 is that it comes precisely at the moment when he has been describing the extraordinary grief and anxiety which his ministry had brought him! At the very moment when he is describing the anguish of ministry, he says, "But thanks be to God, who in Christ always leads us in triumph!" He does not resume his story about the news from Corinth until 7:5.

Paul's claim to victory seems to be so inappropriate in verse 14 that many serious students of the Bible have suggested that 2:14—7:4 is an independent unit which was not written at the same time as the description of Paul's anxiety over the church in chapters 2 and 7. The change in mood is remarkable. We are amazed that these verses, expressing the very different moods of anxiety and triumph, stand together.

Perhaps we have exaggerated the contrast between verses 13 and 14. Paul does not describe himself as the victorious general who leads the triumphal processional. He is himself "led in triumph" as one of the prisoners. As a prisoner in this victorious processional, he is "always" on public display. By his ministry, he "spreads" the knowledge of God. Paul's gratitude that he can have the prisoner's role in this victory processional leads him to exclaim, "Thanks be to God!"

If we understand Paul's role in God's triumphal processional, we may not be shocked at the relationship between verses 13 and 14. It is likely that it is through the anguish and pain of his ministry, as it is described in 1:8-11 and 2:1-13, that Paul sees God's victory processional take place. He knows that his anxiety for the churches is not a lost cause, but is part of a drama that ends in victory. He is grateful to be a prisoner in this cause.

Paul's description of his role in God's victory processional is reminiscent of the powerful image which he employs in 1 Corinthians 4:9: "For I think that God has exhibited us apostles as last of all, like men sentenced to death; because we have become a spectacle to the world, to angels and to men." Since the Greek word for "spectacle" is *theatron*, we might render Paul's word, "We have become a theater to the world." The words remind us that Jesus Himself was a kind of "spectacle" to the crowds who saw His crucifixion. He died as a public example and symbol of humiliation. Paul's words in 1 Corinthians 4:9 indicate that the servant of Christ is willing to share Jesus' fate and become a "spectacle."

One of the major themes in 2 Corinthians is Paul's claim that his ministry is characterized by his sharing in the death of Christ. Just as God is the One who "always" leads him in triumph, Paul is "always" carrying in the body the death of Jesus (4:10). He is willing to share the "weakness" of Christ (13:4; cf. 11:10). But if a major theme is the weakness of the apostle, this theme is accompanied by the claim that God's power is present in weakness: "'. . . my power is made perfect in weakness.' . . . when I am weak, then I am strong" (12:9, 10). Paul's anguish is actually God's victory processional, for he is God's prisoner.

There is a distinct possibility that our exclamation, "Thanks be to God, who always leads us in triumph," will lack the depth and the experience which Paul communicated. We can enjoy the thrill of the words without their context. The victories we seek may be those which seek to avoid the anguish which accompanies our service to God. We may not seek cheap and sensational victories which do not grow out of the pain of the cross. Our models for victory may be derived from the marketplace rather than the cross. While Paul proclaimed a strange kind of victory, it was a distinctively Christian victory that grew out of the cross.

The first reaction which we often have after assuming a responsibility in the church is our dismay at the incredible number of problems confronting us: the energy we spend keeping the peace, the efforts we put into ministering to apathetic Christians, and the routine jobs which are not very exciting. None of these roles, we assume, look like a victory processional. We are usually unprepared for the grief which accompanies this work. But Paul suggests that God's power can be at work through our thankless tasks. We, too, have a role in the victory processional.

In many instances, we may live in the confidence that our ministries are a part of God's victory processional, even if we cannot use the signs of this victory. Every Christian leader has had enough disappointments to raise questions and doubts about the certainty of any victory in which he is involved. The people we count on may disappoint us, and the effort we put into encouraging another may bear no visible result. But victorious moments can come which bring real joy. Indeed, Paul's "Thanks be to God, who always leads us in triumph" may interrupt his story of anguish because he knew that his restless spirit (7:5) was finally calmed and encouraged when Titus brought the good news that the Corinthians had not disappointed Paul. He says, ". . . as he told us of your longing, your mourning, your zeal for me; so that I rejoiced still more" (7:7). Paul's ministry had brought the joy in seeing some results from his labor.

THE AROMA OF CHRIST

The victory processional was an extraordinary spectacle which, like a parade, communicated with delightful visual images. The uniformed generals and the standards held by the soldiers carried a strong visual message. But there was, in addition to the "spectacle," the "smell" of victory. The burning of incense filled the air with smells which gave the message of victory to the populace. The imagery allows Paul to say that the "smell of victory" was in the air in his ministry, and that he was playing an important role.

The imagery of perfumes played an important role in the Bible and other Jewish literature. At times God's Word was compared to a perfume. In many other instances, it is said that sacrifices offered to God were a pleasing aroma (see Genesis 2:21; Exodus 29:12; Leviticus 1:9). Thus it was said in the New Testament that the sacrifice of Christ was a "fragrant offering" to God (Ephesians 5:2). According to verse 14, this "fragrance of the knowledge of him" is being spread in the world. Wherever the story of Jesus is told, this "smell of victory" is being spread. The story of his cross is for Christians the mighty power of God for salvation (1 Corinthians 1:13-25; cf. Romans 1:14-17). Thus the fragrance that is being spread communicates life and power to those who are being saved (2:16), even if it carries the odor of defeat to those who perish (2:16).

The issue of 2 Corinthians is the messenger and his role in this decisive event. Paul is on the defensive, responding to those who claim that he is too weak and incompetent, if not also too dishonest, to carry on a serious ministry. Paul knows that Jesus is not alone the divine fragrance. At times, as he says to the Philippians, our little contribution and gifts are a "fragrant offering" and an "acceptable sacrifice" to God (Philippians 4:18). Our entire lives may be a "living sacrifice" to God (Romans 12:1). Paul makes this point in a graphic way in Philippians 2:17 when he describes himself as being "poured as a libation upon the sacrificial offering of your faith, . . ." Christ's messengers are also poured out as a sacrifice.

To those who questioned Paul's integrity and credentials, his astonishing claim is that he has the important role in God's victory processional. Paul both "spreads the fragrance" (*osme*, 2:14) of the Christian story and is "the aroma" (*euodia*, 2:15) of Christ. Wherever Paul shares this cross of Christ, pouring himself out for others, he shares with his Lord the "smell of victory" and the fragrance that ascends to God.

It was an astonishing claim to be God's instrument in the one great victory processional which mattered. Consequently, Paul asks, "Who is sufficient [*hikanos*] for these things?" The obvious answer is, "No one." The question comes from one who is overwhelmed with the responsiblity that is too great for him. He knows that to be God's aroma is an awesome responsibility. Paul provides his own answer to the question in 3:5, 6: ". . . our competence [*hikanotes*, literally, "sufficiency"] is from God, who has made us competent to be ministers of a new covenant, . . ."

ON NOT BEING HUCKSTERS

If Paul had not been on the defensive, he might not have told about his special place in spreading God's aroma. His real concern, as 2:17 shows, is to answer the charge that he was a "peddler" of God's Word. Paul's denial in this verse suggests that he, like every Christian leader, has to overcome the doubts about his sincerity.

Paul's word for "peddlers" (*kapeleuontes*) was the common word for the retail merchant who bought his wares from the wholesaler and resold them at a profit. Because the retail merchants often increased their profits by misrepresenting the quality of the goods, the word carried the connotation of "huckstering." At times the word was used for the wine merchants who diluted their product with water. Philosophers used the word for those teachers who sold their message for money, at times falsifying and diluting the message if it were to their personal benefit. There were, therefore, "hucksters" in retail trade and "hucksters" who claimed to teach the truth. The one characteristic of the huckster was that he had no personal engagement in his product. It was greed and ambition, not his devotion, which led him to his product.

The New English Bible renders 2:17 appropriately: "We do not go hawking the word of God about." There were, undoubtedly, hucksters of the Word, for whom the story of Christ was a thing to be sold and from which they hoped to profit. There will always be those who are themselves "for sale." This condition exists wherever men lose the sense of awe and wonder at the work in which they are engaged. Our ministries become the equivalent of any other task if we have lost sight of the "smell of victory" in God's service. For those who see themselves as God's captives in a triumphal processional, it is unthinkable to "have the word of God" for profit.

CONCLUSION

The answer to the cynicism about ministry in our time is to catch the vision of our place in God's plan. It is through the personal sacrifices of all of God's servants that the aroma of the story is spread. We are not involved in some trivial enterprise; the aroma which we spread is a matter of life and death. The pain and grief we share is a sharing in the cross of Christ. The role we play in our limited sphere may seem to show no results. But it is a part of spreading the fragrance of the knowledge of Him "in every place" (2:14).

Men become hucksters when they see no particular glory in their work. But no one who is really "captured" in Christ's service will ever treat the gospel as wares to be sold. It is unthinkable to "hawk the Word" if that Word is a victorious march which grasps us in its service. The mark of the Christian, therefore, is that he is "caught up" and "taken prisoner" by a cause that is greater than he. The story is not, like the merchant's goods, a thing to be bought and sold. The Christian is "the aroma of Christ," showing by his demeanor that he has been captivated by the story.

4

OUR COMPETENCE IS FROM GOD
(3:4—4:6)

"Since we have such a hope, we are very bold, . . ."
(3:12).

When I watch candidates campaign for public office, I am often amazed at their display of absolute self-confidence in confronting the country's most serious problems. No candidate, though, would achieve the confidence of the voters if he did not display confidence in his capacity to meet these problems. Therefore, he is expected to tell us, without sounding arrogant, that he can meet challenges such as inflation, unemployment, etc. Many serious thinkers may tell us that the problems are beyond man's reach, but the candidate exhibits the confidence that he is capable of meeting the challenge, whatever it is.

We are a people who admire the confident spirit which boldly says that no task is too big. Many of us hear commercials in the media for self-help courses that are designed to build our confidence. One such course claims to help us "discover the hidden resources" that will lead to our success in practically any task. As we watched the movie, *The Sound of Music*, we were amused at Maria's triumphant spirit after she was told of her new responsibility as governess in a large and difficult household. To our delight, she went to the job singing, "I have confidence in me."

While it is true few challenges can be met without a confidence in our capability, it is also true that self-confidence can become distorted and dangerous. The self-confidence of the public leader may lead him to overestimate his own power and to have an absurd trust in his own capabilities. The self-help course may imply that confidence is a goal in itself without suggesting that it matters how it is applied. The underlying assumption may be that self-confidence is the key to advancing ourselves, and not any particular cause. Thus, there is danger in the words of Maria's song, "I have confidence in me."

Confidence is an important factor in the ministry of the church. A certain kind of confidence is necessary for the teacher, the elder, and the deacon. But it matters what kind of confidence we display. Some people respond to calls for leadership by being overwhelmed by the task. They rightly see that involvement in God's cause demands the best. Because God's cause is so extraordinarily demanding, they avoid assuming responsibility. Others approach an important task with total assurance in their own capacities. They assume that the same boldness that works in the business and professional worlds is appropriate in Christian service. They assume that church leadership, like any other kind of leadership, is a matter of "selling ourselves." Both approaches are distortions of the Christian approach, as 2 Corinthians suggests.

In chapter 3, Paul affirms his confidence to the Corinthian church: "Such is the confidence that we have through Christ toward God" (3:4). Later, he says, "... we are very bold" (3:12). An important issue in this book on ministry is, therefore, the confidence, boldness, and freedom (3:7) of the minister who refuses to be intimidated by the task before him. The mark of the Christian is his confidence in fulfilling his role.

WHAT KIND OF CONFIDENCE (3:4-6)

Paul wrote those words, apparently, because others had suggested that he had no reason to be confident about his work. Others called themselves "servants of Christ" (11:23) who had come to Corinth with unlimited self-confidence. According to 3:1, they came with "letters of recommendation" which described their great works. The fact that they would constantly "commend themselves" (10:12) shows that they were not lacking in self-confidence. Evidently, they had said that Paul's own failure to bring a letter of recommendation was an indication that he had no confidence in his work. Thus, they measured themselves with others, never doubting their capacity to minister.

In response to this kind of self-confidence, Paul insists, "Such is the confidence that we have through Christ toward God" (3:4). His was a different kind of confidence from that of the false teachers, for he says, "Not that we are competent of ourselves to claim anything as coming from us; . . ." (3:5; NRSV). God's cause is far too great for any human servants to be capable of executing His plans. Probably the opponents, in their letters of recommendation, had claimed to be competent for the task. This feature is the unique fact about our confidence in the Christian ministry. We are aware of our personal incompetence; yet we have confidence in our ministries.

Paul's word for "competent" (*hikanos*) was important in his discussion with the Corinthians, probably because some claimed to be "competent." After Paul had spoken of God's triumphant cause, he asked, "And who is sufficient [*hikanos*] for these things?" (2:16). The implied answer was, "No one." Others had probably observed the glaring weaknesses in Paul's speaking ability and his fragile health and concluded that he was "not competent." Paul fully accepted the charge.

The irony is that Paul admits the charge that he is not competent, but still speaks of his confidence. The reason is that "our competence is from God, who has made us competent to be ministers of a new covenant, not in a written code but in the Spirit; for the written code kills, but the Spirit gives life" (3:5, 6). Paul's confidence does not come from his own personal gifts and powers; he knows that God's power has called him and that God can use him in His plan.

God has always done His work through His "servants" or "ministers," most of whom had no outstanding personal charisma. Moses, the "minister" of the old covenant, had serious doubts about his qualifications (cf. Exodus 4:10). Yet God "made him competent" to speak and act for Him. Amos insisted that he was neither a prophet nor a son of a prophet (Amos 7:14). Nevertheless, they were capable because God "made them competent." Paul's competence grew out of the assurance that God could use him in a decisive cause.

This cause had been announced centuries ago by Jeremiah, who described a new day when God would "make a new covenant with the house of Israel and the house of Judah" (Jeremiah 31:31). This covenant, unlike the old one that was written on stone, would be written "on their heart" (Jeremiah 31:33). Paul's extraordinary claim is that he is the "minister" of that covenant as surely as Moses was the minister of the old covenant. Indeed, his readers are his letter of recommendations, a letter "written . . . on tablets of human hearts" (3:3), "delivered" (3:3; literally, "ministered") by Paul. That is, already he has seen the results of his work. As God's "delivery man" or "minister" of the new covenant, he has already seen lives changed through his work. A church with God's will "written on its heart" came to life through Paul. Consequently, he says, "Such is the confidence that we have through Christ toward God." It was different from the popular idea of "self-confidence."

Paul's kind of confidence avoided both the popular (and the opponents') version of self-reliance and the opposite distortion of being overwhelmed by a task that seems too large. Both versions are current temptations to be church and are equally devastation. We are commonly under pressure to cite statistics which, like the letters of recommendation in 3:1, list our achievements. Like the men of the tower of Babel, who wished to "make a name for themselves" (Genesis 11:4), churches may engage in the kind of public relations which will build up their esteem among others and "sell themselves." Competence can be measured by the standards at work in the rest of our society. We may measure missionaries, teachers, evangelists, and others only by artificial standards of success. Paul's response to the self-reliance of others would be helpful for the church. Our confidence is not in our capabilities, but in the fact that God "has made us competent to be ministers." We "rely not on ourselves but on God who raises the dead" (1:9).

A LESSON FROM THE OLD TESTAMENT(3:7-16)

Although Paul often quotes the Old Testament in establishing his point, he rarely uses it for an extended lesson. Therefore, we are surprised in 3:7-16 that, in the middle of Paul's defense of his ministry, he derives a lengthy lesson from the Old Testament. He recalls the occasion when Moses, after talking with God on Mount Sinai, came down the mountain with a radiant face (Exodus 34:29-35). The story suggested fully the glory and power of Moses which set him apart from others. It had been told throughout the centuries by the rabbis to show Moses' unique glory. The fact that Moses had worn the veil when he was in the presence of the people indicated the awesomeness of his ministry. Paul chooses the story of that glorious ministry in order to speak of his own work.

We cannot be sure why Paul chose to derive a lesson from that story in this particular place. He does not refer to it anywhere else. It is possible that the opponents had been claiming to be glorious like Moses. By the standard of Moses' mighty acts and remarkable appearance, Paul was nothing. His ministry was, by comparison, unimpressive. The comparison to Moses should humiliate Paul and show him that his ministry was feeble and inglorious. Moses' ministry was filled with mighty works and power. Even if others might have been modeling themselves after Moses, Paul does not deny the glory of Moses' ministry. Indeed, the word "splendor" (*doxa*; NIV, "glory") occurs repeatedly in 3:7-11 for the "ministry" in which Moses was engaged. Paul reads the Old Testament and knows that it is from God. There was a shining radiance about the story because the glory was from God. The ministry then was no human creation. Moses' shining face was a reminder that, behind this man's work, there was divine power.

Christians need to recall that they understand their task only when they are rooted in the Old Testament. The early church never wished to sever the New Testament from the Old Testament. Our service to God is the continuation of the ministry of

Moses. Therefore, we listen to the "word of the Lord" as it was delivered through the prophets. We recognize, as Paul did, that the first covenant "came with such splendor" (3:7). It is filled with such power that we know that we would be impoverished without this great light.

An infinitely more brilliant glory is described in 3:7-11. While Paul concedes that the ministry of Moses came with splendor, he shows that the Spirit's ministry has greater glory. The awesomeness of Moses as he descended the mountain was nothing compared to Paul's ministry. Unlike the earlier one, this ministry is God's final light shining in the world's darkness. It has the power to change lives and restore them to "righteousness" (3:9). While the earlier light shone brightly, it has lost its luster in comparison with the greater light (3:10). This lesson from the Bible is not only an interesting exercise for Paul. He knows that his ministry is under attack, and he is challenged to show why he goes on with his seemingly fruitless effort with a troublesome church. In this lesson from the Old Testament, Paul is comparing ministries. The RSV "dispensation" (*diakonia*) is best rendered "ministry" (as in the NIV). Paul knows that he has been called to be God's minister in a task more glorious than that of Moses. Others claim that he is incompetent to be a minister because of his lack of "charisma" and glory. But he knows that the new kind of ministry has a different kind of glory from what others expect. He is God's agent in the most important movement in the world.

Paul's opponents undoubtedly said that the "glory" of their work—the emphasis on spectacular achievements and experiences—was visible, like Moses' shining face. But Paul points to another way of measuring glory. There is even glory in a cross. The church needs to be reminded that God has called His people to a different kind of glory that manifests the cross to others.

The observer in ancient times would have wondered, along with the Corinthian church, how an unimpressive person like Paul could speak with such certainty. Paul concludes from the story of Moses, "Since we have such a hope, we are very bold" (3:12). He is not intimidated by the task. "Boldness" (*parrhe-*

sia) is the major characteristic of Paul's ministry. The dominant tone of chapter 3 is that this man whose credentials have been questioned is "confident" (3:4) and "bold" (3:12) and "free" (3:17). Even when others challenge his ministry, he is free. He does not alter his message to suit prevailing tastes, nor does he remain quiet before those who are unconvinced.

Paul's word for "boldness" was an important one among public figures in the ancient world. The word means "freedom of speech." It described the demeanor of the wise man who fearlessly stood before a king or a tyrant and told the truth, even if it was unpleasant. The story is told that Diogenes, the founder of the Cynic school, was once visited by Alexander the Great, who asked the philosopher if the great general could do anything for him. His reply was, "Stand a little out of my sun." Because he was so sure of his message, he was known for his absolute freedom and boldness.

Paul spoke with freedom (3:7) and boldness (3:12) because of the glory of his ministry. Moses had used the veil to conceal from Israel the fading of the glory of his ministry (3:13), leaving many confused and "veiled" in their understanding even in Paul's day. Some, including those who boasted of their accomplishments, still have the veil "over their minds" (3:14, 15) because they have not recognized the greater glory of the new covenant. To them, with their limited perspective, Paul's confidence is foolish, and his ministry is unimpressive. But Paul has the freedom of one who "turns to the Lord" (3:16, 17) to see a greater glory. Nothing is so liberating as the truth. He says, "But when a man turns to the Lord the veil is removed" (3:16). This encounter with Christ makes us free: ". . . where the Spirit of the Lord is, there is freedom" (3:17).

ON BEING TRANSFORMED (3:18)

This extraordinary freedom is experienced when "we all, with unveiled face, beholding the glory of the Lord, are being changed into his likeness from one degree of glory to another; . . ." (3:18). Moses alone was changed by his encounter with God. Now "we all"—Paul and the entire church—are being made more like Him. "We shall be like him," we are told in 1 John 3:2. The word for "changed" is the striking Greek word *metamorpheo* which has come into the English language as "metamorphosis." The word suggests that a Christian experiences a "change of form" or "change of shape" as he beholds Christ. We are told to "be transformed" (*metamorpheo*) by the renewing of our minds (Romans 12:2). In Galatians 4:19, Paul says, ". . . until Christ be formed in you."

The Christian is "shaped" by what he beholds. If we behold Christ's glory, we will, like Moses, be changed into that glory. The word for "behold" (*katoptrizomai*) is a strong word that was used for "gazing" or "contemplating" in a mirror. The word suggests the steady gaze and careful contemplation of those who looked at the image in a pool of water or in an imperfect mirror. The word, with its idea of an intent gaze, is appropriate for the Christian's contemplation of Christ.

What we behold shapes us. If we behold what is shameful, we will reflect the shame. If like Paul's opponents, we are shaped by the values of our culture, we will measure our programs by the same standards that are used in the marketplace. The church will be left with nothing to say. It will only be a reflection of others. But if our steady gaze is fixed on the shining light of the Man who gave Himself for others, we will be changed into His kind of glory. If we are changed by Him, we can share Paul's confidence, boldness, and freedom.

If Christians are "transformed" by what they gaze at intently, this will be a distinguishing mark of the Christian. We will all be shaped by the story of selfless love. We will seek out leaders who have had the opportunity to "behold the glory of God" long enough to reflect the story on their lives. Our ministries will be judged by one criterion: that they reflect the intent of the One who came to serve.

CONCLUSION

Once a devout believer was summoned before a Nazi court during Hitler's reign. As the believer answered the questions about his activities truthfully, it occurred to him that he was the only free person in the room. The magistrates and the SS troops were themselves living in dread. Their faces betrayed their anxiety. The one who was free was the believer who served another Lord. This fact gave him the confidence to speak.

Confidence is a mark of the Christian. It is not self-confidence, but the knowlege that we have seen a glory that liberates us from reflecting the values of our culture. We can speak boldly for God because "our competence is from God" (3:5).

5

KNOCKED DOWN, BUT NOT KNOCKED OUT
(4:7-15)

"... to show that the transcendant power belongs to
God...." (4:7).

Many years ago, my family and I were going through the
Louvre Museum, admiring some of the greatest art treasures in
the world. We came to a crowd which had gathered around one
of the paintings. This painting was enclosed in a glass case. A
guard stood nearby. As we came close enough to see the
painting, we recognized the famous *Mona Lisa*. Among the
many art treasures in this majestic hall, it was the priceless
treasure. It was protected against theft, vandalism, and the
touch of admirers. The protection behind a glass seemed to be
the only appropriate way to preserve an irreplaceable work of
art.

I have often noticed the elaborate precautions taken by
museums to preserve their treasures. Thousands of people who
filed by to see the treasures of King Tut saw the effort which
had gone into protecting those artifacts behind glass cases. No
responsible person would allow a three-thousand-year-old
treasure to be defaced by someone's thoughtless act. In museums everywhere, if paintings are not secured by glass cases,
they are protected by electronic security devices which sound
whenever they are touched. Treasures of all kinds, whether in
museums or homes, require special treatment, for it is tragic to
observe the deterioration of a priceless object.

39

This fact suggests the shocking effect of Paul's words in 4:7: "We have this treasure in earthen vessels, . . ." The earthen vessel in Paul's day was the inexpensive clay pot. Archaeologists who dig in ancient cities like Corinth find thousands of fragments of these clay pots and jars. These "nonbiodegradable" objects were the items most often left behind, perhaps because they were both plentiful and cheap. As these countless fragments demonstrate, the pots and jars were particularly fragile. They were useful as containers for food, but no one would have ever considered placing a treasure in one of them. Treasures belonged in something that was secure against the forces of nature or of human greed. Thus when Paul said, "We have this treasure in earthen vessels," he was describing an extraordinary sight.

THE TREASURE

The treasure which "we have" is the ministry of the gospel. In the context of our passage, Paul has spoken of a light that "shone in our hearts to give the light of the knowledge of the glory of God in the face of Christ" (4:6). The "light" is the proclamation that Jesus Christ is Lord (4:5). When Paul speaks of the treasure "we have," a special emphasis is placed on the fact that the treasure was given to us. Several times, he speaks of blessings which Christians "have" (3:4, 12; 4:1). In each instance, he says that these blessings come to us as gifts. He says in 4:1, "Having this ministry by the mercy of God, . . ." In the same way, God's treasure is ours because God placed it in our hands.

The "treasure" is a favorite image in the Bible for the good news of the gospel. Jesus once said that "the kingdom of heaven is like treasure hidden in a field" (Matthew 13:44). He told a twin parable in which the kingdom was compared to "one pearl of great value" (Matthew 13:46). Paul wrote that in Christ "are hid all the treasures of wisdom and knowledge" (Colossians 2:3). This image was used commonly because it communicated an important fact about the gospel: The gospel is of such extraordinary value that no one can take it lightly.

It is no accident that the gospel is compared to a treasure, and not a cheap trinket. When the man in the parable found the treasure and the pearl, he sold all that he had to have the one thing. The parable suggested the infinite value of the gospel. When we discover it, we find the treasure for which we are willing to sacrifice everything.

In the National Museum of Athens, Greece, some remarkable treasures of gold date back to the twelfth century B.C., the period which had long been described in the legends about the Trojan War. In the latter part of the nineteenth century, Heinrich Schliemann unearthed these treasures after being told repeatedly that he could never find the relics of that heroic age. Although he had little idea of the magnificence of the treasures he would find, the idea was the passion of his life. He himself spent a fortune on the archaeological discoveries, for nothing motivated him as much as did the dream of the Greek treasure.

Jesus was aware that we all have a treasure. We choose either the treasure on earth that can be stolen or corrupted or the one in heaven which no one can take away. "For where your treasure is," He said, "there will your heart be also" (Matthew 6:21). Paul was certain that we, with our ministry to Christ, "have this treasure."

The mark of the Christian is the recognition that a treasure has been placed in his hands. We face the constant temptation not to take our ministries seriously because we expect very little from them. The repetition of many tasks, as well as the low esteem in which they are held, turns ministries into monotonous jobs. There are few congregations in which important ministries—visiting the hospitals, caring for the unfortunate, working with the visitation team—do not die a slow death. The enthusiasm often diminishes after the beginning.

What is lacking in many instances is the reminder that we have a treasure in these activities. If our treasure is with our ministry, we will certainly not allow the other demands to rob us of our commitment to an important ministry. James S. Stewart, the well-known Scottish preacher, has asked the appropriate question: What does the church need most today for its evangelistic mission? He answers,

More modern techniques, no doubt, more up-to-date methods, more contemporary structures of church life, more brand-new machinery. But basically the need is surely this: a far deeper sense of the riches we possess, a far livelier appropriation of the supernatural, transcendent resources that we always present to faith in a Risen Lord.[1]

Not long ago, I heard a woman comment on her husband's involvement in the programs of the church. She explained his involvement by saying that he had not grown up in a Christian environment. Only when he became an adult did he discover the gospel and a local congregation of Christians. Because he had never taken the Christian life for granted, it meant something special to him! To use Paul's language, that man had found the treasure. The problem with our approach to many problems of the church is that they have become common to us. Those who live with the treasure for a long time may forget its real value. Those who see it afresh often recognize its value for their lives.

IN EARTHEN VESSELS

The earthen vessel holding the treasure is obviously the Christian servant, with his weaknesses, imperfections, and fragility. God did not choose to place His treasures in a fortress or in the sturdiest and most secure glass case. God's treasure was placed in fragile earthenware jars.

The image of the earthen vessel is so appropriate for our fragile lives that it is often employed in the Bible to remind us of our own weaknesses. The psalmist says, "I have become like a broken vessel" (Psalms 31:12). Jeremiah describes a man as a "despised, broken pot" (Jeremiah 22:28). But even though our lives are as fragile as an earthen vessel, the prophets remind us regularly that God is the skilled workman who can put the fragile pot to good use. God works with the clay and shapes it for His own purpose (Jeremiah 18:1-11; cf. Isaiah 29:16; 45:9).

---

[1]James S. Steward, *The Wind of the Spirit* (Nashville, Tenn.: Abingdon Press, 1975), 19.

The clay, in its weakness, has no right to resist the potter's will (cf. Romans 9:19, 20), for he can take the worthless clay and use it as his instrument.

Paul's statement that "we have this treasure in earthen vessels" is so vivid that we easily forget its original context. Paul probably would not have made this comment if he had not been the target of stinging criticism. His opponents questioned his authenticity on the grounds that he was too weak to be an authentic minister. "His letters are weighty and strong," they said, "but his bodily presence is weak, and his speech of no account" (10:10). It was as if they had said, "We expected an orator as electrifying as the orators in the public places." Perhaps they were saying, "We expected someone handsome and godlike, like the athletes of the Olympian games." Paul, the proclaimer of the Word of God, was hardly what the sophisticated Corinthians had expected in a leader. His response was the reminder that God had deliberately chosen to place His treasure in fragile earthen vessels, not in powerful and unblemished containers.

Paul once made a similar argument in 1 Corinthians when he attempted to convince the Corinthians that God does not conform to human standards. Indeed, God chose to make Himself known through a cross, the symbol of shame and weakness. Then Paul added, "For consider your call, brethren; not many of you were wise according to worldly standards, not many were powerful, not many of noble birth" (1 Corinthians 1:26). The whole church was composed of "earthen vessels"— people who had no power of their own. God did not need the wise, the powerful, and the noble to carry out His work.

If we forget that God's treasure is placed in "earthen vessels," we create serious problems for the church. In our culture, with its esteem for media stars of every kind, we become saturated with the view that "superstars" are necessary for important tasks. In recent years, one major evangelistic movement has made a special point of showing that glamorous media stars commend the faith. The assumption seems to be that the presence of extraordinary talent gives credibility to the faith.

If we forget that God has chosen to place His treasure in

earthen vessels, we lose patience with those who lead us. We are quick to identify the "incompetence" of the elders or the mediocrity of the minister's sermons, and then to conclude that the church's future would be greatly enhanced if every worship service were as slick as a television special. We conclude that the church could be healthy if only we found someone of genuine "star" quality.

On one occasion, several members of a congregation were complaining that their minister was "so average" that he should resign, for he was the cause of the church's failures. A wiser member replied, "Yes, but we are an 'average' congregation." Most congregations are. The level of competence may not approach that of the corporation. The execution of the programs may lack the desired efficiency, and the staff may not measure well against others. But I am convinced that, if Paul's words are taken seriously, we will recall that the whole church is composed of breakable jars.

This recognition should give us patience for the mistakes which we perceive in others. Practically all who have involved themselves seriously have made serious mistakes which they regret. Often we lack sufficient foresight to anticipate the results of our decisions. We have made indiscreet comments which, upon reflection, we should have withheld. Being a community of "earthen vessels" involves some human failures. A church which recalls this fact will exercise patience.

Since we are a community of "earthen vessels," there is also a place for our patience with those who have committed serious moral offenses. There is a spirit which will never forget a lapse which lies far in the distant past. We may act as though the offense forever disqualifies another from participation in any program. But such a spirit ignores the fact that God can use as His "chosen instruments" those who have committed serious offenses. He even used one who had persecuted the church.

The fact that God has chosen to use "earthen vessels" does not suggest that we accept our incompetence and our failures without making the effort to commit ourselves totally to the task. It would be a distortion of Paul's message to assume that, because God has chosen fallible people as His instruments, He does not demand from us an intense commitment and the best we have to offer. Authentic ministry involves the security of knowing that God can use breakable jars like us, but it does not mean that we accept our limitations complacently and without any effort to improve. It is true that God can use the mediocre speaker and the one who has no special talent for administering and organizing. But the recognition that we hold a treasure keeps us from becoming apathetic and complacent.

TO SHOW THAT THE POWER BELONGS TO GOD

If only "superstars" were capable of rendering service to God, we might mistake the source of the power. But if God works through earthen vessels, the power is obviously His. The word "power" (*dynamis*) occurs several times in 1 and 2 Corinthians (cf. 1 Corinthians 1:18, 24; 2:5; 2 Corinthians 12:9; 13:4), perhaps in response to men who boasted of their own power to do extraordinary things. Paul regularly reminds his brethren that God has chosen to exhibit His in human weakness (12:9; 13:4), for then God's power is unmistakable. It was in the weakness of the cross that God's power was most evident.

James S. Stewart has told about the work of D. L. Moody in Birmingham, England. When Moody was preaching in a missionary campaign, a skeptical observer came to the meeting night after night watching the methods of the evangelist with a critical eye. Eventually, he went to Moody and said, "I have seen this mission of yours, and have come to the conclusion that it is truly of God. I'll tell you why. It is because I can see no possible relation between you personally and the results your mission is achieving. Therefore, it must be of God!"[2]

Paul suggests that God can use us, not in spite of our infirmities, but because of them. If we take Paul's message seriously, we are likely to find a distinct danger of being infected by the world's standards of strength and of our trying to build the kingdom by our own resourcefulness. This mistake had been committed by Paul's opponents in their constant

---

[2]Ibid., 23.

insistence on their own gifts. Authentic ministry involves our admission that God is the creative potter who can use us to His glory.

KNOCKED DOWN, BUT NOT KNOCKED OUT
(4:8-15)

That Paul is a breakable jar is made clear in the poetic lines in 4:8, 9. Four parallel phrases illustrate his life as an earthen vessel. In the first half of each phrase, he describes his fragile condition. He is "afflicted," "perplexed," "persecuted," and "struck down." These words suggest the defenselessness of one who is powerless against the forces which crush him. He recognizes that he has no resources of his own. These phrases are similar to other passages where Paul lists those sufferings which "commend" him as an authentic disciple (6:4-6; 11:23-29). He is known for his weakness, not his remarkable powers.

Paul's intention is not to emphasize his many trials, for each time he refers to an ordeal of his ministry, he follows with the phrase, "but not." That is, he has been helpless, but never defeated. Despite his lack of resources, he was never beaten. He recalled specific examples where God had rescued him when he had seemed most helpless (cf. 1:8-11). Paul's statement that he was "afflicted . . . but not crushed" reminds us of the numerous references to the endurance of afflictions (1:4, 8; 2:4; 4:17; 6:4). The word for "affliction" (*thlipsis*) connotes being "jammed" or "pressed" so hard that he was "crushed." The NIV renders the verse appropriately: "We are hard pressed on every side, but not crushed." The mark of the Christian is not the absence of pain, but the fact that he is not destroyed by it.

Paul is also "not driven to despair," "not forsaken," and "not destroyed." In one sense, Paul had "despaired" (1:8), but not in the sense that he had given up forever. He shares with other biblical writers the conviction that, while others forsake us (2 Timothy 4:10, 16), God does not. God says, "I will never fail you nor forsake you" (Hebrews 13:5). He knew that many times we, as "earthen vessels," are "knocked down." We are the victims of numerous attacks on our work. But we are not "destroyed." J. B. Phillips renders the last phrase of 4:8, "knocked down but not knocked out." Authentic Christianity is characterized, therefore, by the spirit which says confidently, "but not"—not crushed, not despairing, not forsaken, and not destroyed. This "but not" grows out of our conviction that God's power works in His earthen vessels.

One of the most remarkable features in 2 Corinthians is Paul's frequent reminder that his sufferings "commend" him as a true servant of Christ (6:4; 11:23-29; 1:8-11). Paul says that his weakness demonstrates that he is "carrying in the body the death of Jesus" (4:10), for Jesus had Himself been a defenseless man who was persecuted and struck down. To His enemies, Jesus had been weak and ridiculous. He was, according to Paul, "crucified in weakness" (13:4). Jesus had been, like His servants, a "breakable jar" who suffered pain and who died. The authentic Christian's pain and weakness are a sharing in the fate of Jesus. Paul speaks often of his sharing in Jesus' suffering (Philippians 3:10; Galatians 2:20; 6:17).

Paul seems to say that there is no shame in the servant's weakness and fragility. Paul, with his many weaknesses, could have developed an inferiority complex. Some were like "stars" by comparison to him. But Paul recalls that Jesus Himself was fragile. To the eyes of many in Jerusalem, Jesus was very ordinary. The soldiers who ridiculed Him had seen no special power or glory in Him.

The great Russian novelist Ivan Turgenev described a vision in which he came to understand the humanity of Jesus:

> I saw myself, a youth, almost a boy, in a low-pitched wooden church. There stood before me many people, all fair-haired peasant heads. From time to time, they began swaying, falling, rising again, like the ripe ears of wheat when the wind in summer passes over them. All at once a man came up from behind and stood beside me. I did not turn towards him, but I felt that the man was Christ. Emotion, curiosity, awe overmastered me. I made an effort and looked at my neighbor. A face like everyone's, a face like all men's faces.

"What sort of Christ is this?" I thought. "Such an ordinary, ordinary man. It cannot be." He could not grasp that the face of Christ was like the face of all men. The wonder of the incarnation is that God chose to speak through a man—an earthen vessel, not a "superman" who turned stones to bread, jumped from temples, or forced people to follow.

We need to acknowledge that Jesus chose to "empty himself" (Philippians 2:7) of greatness and to become, in a sense, ordinary. Then we can be prepared to accept the glory of the resurrection, when God's power was demonstrated in the presence of weakness. Paul knows that only when he is fragile can God's resurrection power, His "life" (4:11), be present in his life. Paul's consistent "but not" is the confident word of one who knows that those who share the weakness of Christ also share His power. As Paul says later, "When I am weak, then I am strong" (12:10).

CONCLUSION

The prerequisite to discovering God's power in our ministries is not in acquiring the most influential people in town for our friendship, in having the most talented staff, or in having the most outstanding facilities, for then we might be displaying our power. The mark of the Christian life is not the exercise of political strength, for there also the power would be our own. God's power is present when we risk ourselves and acknowledge that we are earthen vessels. Indeed, God's power was most dramatically shown in the experience of the man who died defenseless at the hands of His enemies.

6

ALWAYS OF GOOD COURAGE
(4:16—5:10)

"For we walk by faith, not by sight" (5:7).

If we were to write a history of our local congregations, using the old bulletins and other records as our resource, one feature would probably be held in common by practically every church. Our records would reveal a pattern of beginning new ministries with great enthusiasm, only to be followed by our "losing heart" after the excitement had worn off. The bus ministry and the visitation program, for example, may attract more volunteers than we can use when the programs are first announced. But frequently, the volunteers dwindle until only a few are left to oversee the programs. They, too, "lose heart" for the task. When a pattern of giving up on vital ministries occurs, we easily become cynical about the prospects for any new ministry.

This pattern has left many capable people "burned out" after years of thinking that they would make the difference. Indeed, I cannot think of any area of the church's many ministries where discouragement is not a critical problem. Those who were put in charge of the bus ministry and the visitation program "lose heart" after an extended period of trying to enlist volunteers for their work. The Sunday school teacher has the same routine for years. Elders and ministers easily tire of a work in which they see only endless problems. Many of us enter programs thinking that we will "make a difference," but later we doubt if we do. I am convinced that the danger to our ministries is not the lack of good ideas or capable people. Our problem is that we "burn out."

If we are honest, we will admit that many ministries in the church are discouraging. It is difficult for the Sunday school teacher to see that he or she is making a difference. The pulpit minister, knowing that he lives in a culture which delights in measuring everything, has few measurable successes. How do you measure transformed lives? How do you know when your effort was decisive in building up the church? Even in churches where there has been considerable numerical growth, spiritual growth is not easily measured. Because our successes are not easy to measure, we demand tangible evidence that our work has made a difference. We point to the new educational wing, the debt-free building, and the attendance record to show our success. But we know that there must be more to a successful ministry then these visible signs.

I have referred to discouragement as "losing heart" because the RSV uses this term in 4:1, 16. This word (*egkakein*) is used often enough in the New Testament to suggest that our congregations are not alone in "losing heart." The frequent advice against losing heart in the New Testament shows that Christians have always grown discouraged. Jesus' parable of the persistent widow who refused to give up in her request to the unjust judge was told in order to encourage the disciples: "He told them a parable, to the effect that they ought always to pray and not lose heart" (Luke 18:1). Apparently, He told this parable because the disciples' prayer for the coming of God's kingdom seemed to be without results.

Often, Paul counseled Christians not to "lose heart." He wrote to both the Galatians (6:9) and the Thessalonians (2 Thessalonians 3:13) telling them not to "be weary [*egkakein*] in well-doing." The Ephesians are told not to "lose heart" because of Paul's suffering. Paul knew, therefore, that ministry is confronted with the temptation to "lose heart."

On two occasions in 2 Corinthians, Paul says, "We do not lose heart" (4:1, 16). The fact that Paul repeats this statement suggests that it is particularly important to him in his discussion with the Corinthians. Evidently, Paul had to answer those who were challenging his ministry and suggesting that he should be discouraged! His weakness, his fragility, and his many defeats should have meant he would himself be a defeated man! By human standards, his ministry was a failure. We do not know how large the church at Corinth was, but we do know that it was troublesome and rebellious. When opponents observed that Paul devoted himself to the point that his health was failing and that there were no signs of success, they claimed that he was a ridiculous figure whose body was "wasting away" (4:16) while he gave himself for a lost cause.

How does one keep from giving in to discouragement? Paul's answers to those who claimed that he should "lose heart" will be helpful to those of us who, like Paul, cannot easily measure our visible successes. In 4:16—5:10, Paul gives the reason why he, without measuring up to the standards of success others imposed, continued his ministry.

WE LOOK NOT TO THE THINGS THAT ARE SEEN (4:16-18)

On the surface, Paul had reasons for "losing heart." His "outer nature" (literally, "outer man") was "wasting away" (4:16). One possible reason for giving up was the constant "affliction." According to many, it was a demonstration that he was a failure. Throughout 2 Corinthians, Paul's physical weakness and affliction have been the issue (cf. 4:7, 8). He is always "dying" for Jesus Christ (4:10, 11; cf. 1 Corinthians 15:31; Romans 8:36). The ministry to which he has been called has given him every reason, in human terms, to be discouraged.

How can one fail to "lose heart" when his efforts are going nowhere? Most of us can tolerate inconvenience and pain if we believe that our work will bring results. It is when we no longer see a future that we want to give up. Perhaps the lingering death of many of our efforts in the church occurs when we see our sacrifices leading nowhere.

Through the eyes of faith, Paul was able to view the relationship between sacrifice and results in a way that encouraged him. The "wasting away" and the afflictions were limited to the "outer nature," the physical body (cf. 12:9ff.). His body, through the stress of his work and the pain inflicted by others, might be in the process of deterioration, but his real self could not be destroyed by the beatings and the sleepless nights. Paul recognized that his sufferings were "slight" (*parautika*) and "momentary" (*elaphron*) The second term suggests that his sufferings are insignificant in comparison with the glory that is eternal. That is, the sufferings are out of proportion to the results because the sufferings are insignificant in comparison with the eternal results of his work.

Anyone who has been involved in a difficult job has felt that the task was "eternal." The years of deprivation when one goes to school to learn a profession may seem eternal at first. I recall difficult summer jobs while I was in college which, I was sure, lasted an eternity. Now that many years have passed, I see how brief those summers were. This kind of perspective prevents Paul from being discouraged. The afflictions of the moment are trivial in comparison with the "eternal weight of glory." Indeed, the pain of the moment is not merely a nuisance to be gotten out of the way. It is "preparing for us" an eternal weight of glory. There is a reason why our ministries do not always have measurable signs of success; our apparent failures prepare us for real results which we cannot see at the present. This belief in the future kept Paul's ministry alive. He wrote to the Romans, "I consider that the sufferings of this present time are not worth comparing with the glory that is to be revealed to us" (Romans 8:18). He asked,

> Who shall separate us from the love of Christ? Shall tribulation, or distress, or persecution, or famine, or nakedness, or peril, or sword? As it is written, "For thy sake we are being killed all the day long; we are regarded as sheep to be slaughtered" (Romans 8:35, 36).

His certainty in a future gave him the confidence to go on without growing discouraged.

If our congregations have a history of programs that failed

and leaders who "lose heart," it is likely that we have been victimized by the impatience of our age. The mentality which says that the sacrifices are too great for the meager results has not grasped Paul's grand picture of the future. Our demand for instant results to prove that our program is "paying off" indicates that our ministries are lacking in faith. There is a danger in an approach which demands visible signs of success. Paul's confident spirit, by contrast, grew out of his assurance of the unseen: "Because we look not to the things that are seen but to the things that are unseen; for the things that are seen are transient, but the things that are unseen are eternal" (4:18).

RENEWAL EVERY DAY

Those who were criticizing Paul's ministry had measured only the "outer nature," and they could see that it was unimpressive in every respect. But something about this minister was "unseen" and impossible to measure. It was the "inner nature" that was being "renewed every day" (4:16). Paul was not only encouraged and strengthened by his convictions about a glorious future. His Christian life was more than a painful ordeal that would exhaust him until that future began. There is an emphasis in 4:16 on what is happening "every day." At the very moment when the "outer nature is wasting away," the "inner nature" is being renewed. Paul knew that the Christian life involved more than an unseen and glorious future; a glorious present is also unseen. Those who insist on measurable results and visible signs may not see what is happening "every day." But Paul knows through faith that the present is also good.

What is taking place every day in the many struggles is what Paul calls "renewal" (4:16). He speaks elsewhere in this letter about the experience that is common to all Christians: the moment when they become "new creations" (5:17). But this moment of becoming "new" through God's power is not limited to that single event. Their "renewal" is continuous; it is a power that enables them to go on. This reference to the part of us that "is being renewed" is similar to the earlier statement that God's servant "is being changed" (3:18). Both instances involve the conviction that the Christian has resources and power that keep him from "losing heart." He knows that "every day" that power equips him for the tasks God assigns.

The New Testament refers to the ongoing renewal of the Christian. Paul writes to the Romans, "Do not be conformed to this world, but be transformed by the renewal of your mind, . . ." (Romans 12:2). ". . . put on the new nature," he writes to the Colossians, "which is being renewed in knowledge after the image of its creator" (Colossians 3:10). Renewal is God's work, not our own. When we believe that the work of ministry depends on our own resources, we fail. We do not "lose heart" when we acknowledge that God has not abandoned us.

An irony can be seen in Paul's statement that, while our "outer nature is wasting away, our inner nature is being renewed every day." He is certain that he is gaining new strength at the very time that his body is losing strength. This new strength belongs to the "inner nature," the part of us that does not "waste away." Our bodies may be subject to all of the pains mentioned in 4:8-10, but this weakness does not affect our inner selves. The "inner nature" (literally, "inner man") is that part of us which thinks and wills. Paul refers to this in Romans 7:22. In Ephesians 3:16, he has a beautiful prayer, that "he [Christ] may grant you to be strengthened with might through his Spirit in the inner man." According to Paul, strength lay in his weakness, for neither a beating nor a sleepless night could exhaust the strength of the part of him which mattered, the part destined for eternity.

The opponents who criticized Paul's ministry had difficulty, no doubt, believing in a power of the inner person that could not be seen and measured. We often feel more comfortable with their demands than with Paul's faith! Inner resources cannot be reported in the church bulletin as visible signs of strength. Nor can we easily prove to anyone else that our ministries are authentic on the basis of inner resources. We share with Paul's critics the desire for the visible signs that will encourage us. Paul's experience of a power that was unobservable prevented him from "losing heart."

If we learn this valuable lesson, we will see our ministries in a radically new way. We will be able to find strength at the very place where we appear to be failures. Ministries that seem to fail will be the occasion for finding new strength. Frustrations in church programs will be the opportunity for us to grow spiritually. The ill health which challenges our faith will allow us to develop spiritual resources. Authentic Christianity looks not for the success of the "outer nature," but to the strength of the "inward nature" which cannot be measured.

WE ARE OF GOOD COURAGE (5:1-10)

In 5:1-10, Paul describes in greater detail those "unseen" and "eternal" things. Graphic images are used to describe them. We have a "building" to replace our flimsy "tent." We will "put on" our "heavenly dwelling" in the same way that we would put on a new set of clothes (5:2). By putting on our new dwelling, we shall never be found "naked" (5:3). The words are not easily understood. Our natural inclination is to use Paul's words about the future in order to produce our own detailed picture of the future life. Paul spoke frequently about his hope for a time when he would go to be with Christ (Philippians 1:23). In 1 Corinthians, he spoke of the return of Christ when those who belong to the Lord will be made alive with him (1 Corinthians 15:23). In 1 and 2 Thessalonians, he graphically described the day of the Lord's return. It is natural for us to wish to know how all of these passages fit together. When do we "put on" our "heavenly dwelling"? In what sense do we "have" this dwelling now? The questions of "how" and "when" have fascinated people of all ages.

In the last decade, we have observed that no subject fascinates large numbers of people as much as does the theme of the end of time. Movies and popular books are distributed to an audience of millions who want to know how and when God will bring our history to a close. It is likely that they are far more interested in speculative questions than was Paul. In the difficult verses in 5:1-4, Paul attempts to describe the indescribable. He wishes to demonstrate the vast difference between the flimsy tent we now inhabit and the dwelling which God has prepared. One belongs to the things that are seen and the other to the unseen world.

The "earthly tent" was an appropriate image for the body. Isaiah 38:12 records the words of King Hezekiah after he had recovered from an illness: "My dwelling is plucked up and removed from me like a shepherd's tent; like a weaver I have rolled up my life; he cuts me off from the loom; from day to night thou dost bring me to an end." Job describes that transient and painful life of those who "dwell in houses of clay" (Job 4:19). The image of the tent suggests how transient our bodily existence is. In fact, Paul describes life in this tent as filled with groaning, sighing, and anxiety (5:2, 4). This "earthly tent" is made of such flimsy material that it is sure to be destroyed (5:1).

Those who criticized Paul's ministry focused on what could be seen—the groaning, the sighing, and the anxiety of one who lived in an "earthly tent." They concluded, upon observing a "tent" that was wearing out, that his ministry was futile. But Paul has a different standard of perception. He says, "For we walk by faith, not by sight" (5:7). He refused to conduct his ministry according to visible standards because he knew that a stable and reliable building would eventually replace the flimsy tent. This building was "not made with hands, eternal in the heavens" (5:1). He could endure the groaning at the present, for he "knew" (5:1) that he possessed this eternal dwelling.

To "walk by faith, not by sight" (5:7) is a mark of the Christian. We, like Paul's opponents, find it easier to "walk by sight." Some prefer to think of the Christian life as if it involved being already "out of this world," far removed from anxiety and frustration. Perhaps Paul's reference in 12:2 to his experience in the third heaven was written precisely because many emphasized that the Christian life was "out of this world." According to 5:1-4, there is another side of the story. We are still waiting and "longing" to put on the heavenly dwelling. While we "walk by faith," we "sigh with anxiety" (5:4). A faith which is based on visible signs is no faith at all (cf. Romans 8:24). Faith involves trusting God when we cannot see the proof of His work in the world. It involves sharing the cross of Jesus when the positive outcome is not in sight. Authentic Christianity includes accepting the anxiety that comes with building our lives on what we cannot see. We know that there is more to come.

Scribbled on a wall of a cellar in Cologne, Germany, during the violence and despair of World War II was a remarkable confession of faith which is similar to that which Paul espoused:

> I believe in the sun, even when it is not shining;
> I believe in love, even when I feel it not;
> I believe in God, even when he is silent.

Paul chose to trust God, even when he could not see the heavenly dwelling.

Paul is saying in 5:1 that "we know" that "we have a building from God," though he could not see it (5:7). He was certain that, while the body (the tent) may be destroyed, we will never "be found naked," for we will "put on" our new set of clothes (5:3). The RSV and NIV reflect accurately the fact that Paul uses three different terms for this new "set of clothes" which we will wear. We have a "building" (*oikodome*), a "house" (*oikia*), and a "dwelling" (*oiketerion*). The words suggest the permanence and superior quality of the future home. They remind us that, although our health may fail, our relationship to God never ceases. We may use many different images to describe our future with God, but behind them all is one certainty: God has promised us a life that will not end. We are serving in a cause which cannot be stopped.

Someone has commented that early Christianity brought hope to a world that had given up hope. According to Ephesians 2:12, these Gentile readers were "without hope" before they became Christians. Those who obeyed Christ were made aware of a future which gave their lives meaning and motivated them to serve. It could be argued that we also face a culture which has given up on hope. Movies and novels commonly portray people who despair of seeing any future worthy of our sacrifice. If we have lost the certainty that "we have a building from God" (5:1), we have lost one of the most vital elements in the Christian life. While it is true that fanatics have often overemphasized this belief in the future through wild and arbitrary speculation, their overemphasis and their many distortions of this belief are no reason for Christians to become embarrassed in expressing this hope. There is an important place for sermons, hymns, and instructions which remind us of our Christian hope. A necessary part of genuine ministry is the willingness to "walk by faith" and not by sight.

CONCLUSION

Paul had no interest in speculating about the future, nor in filling in all of the gaps in the "how" and "when" of the end. He wished to show his critics why he, with his failing health, was never discouraged when his lack of results gave him every reason to be. Paul's attitude was this: to be "always of good courage" (5:6; cf. 5:8). No momentary defeat could discourage the minister who knew that a great future was already guaranteed. The perspective which can say, "We walk by faith, not by sight" is the sign of the authentic Christian.

7

COMFORTED BY GOD
(1:3-11; 7:5-16)

"But God, . . . comforted us by the coming
of Titus" (7:6).

One of the great themes throughout the Bible is the good news that Jesus offers us release from the burdens of life. The New Testament seems to resound with the message that Christians have found "rest for their souls" (cf. Matthew 11:28-50). Those who "bind heavy burdens" (cf. Matthew 23:4) which no one can bear are the legalists who make demands no one can keep. Others are under the oppressive weight of slavery to their impulses, but the Christian has been liberated from his worst instincts. This lifting of the burden is the good news of Christianity.

Another side of the story often comes to the Christian as a surprise. Active discipleship can also be extremely burdensome. From my earliest memory, I recall being present when many burdens of church life were being discussed. One tense moment was followed by another. Many of those moments resulted in disappointing consequences. In other instances, there were the burdens of nurturing those whose commitment never seemed to grow. I have spoken to many active Christians who expressed a disappointment and anguish that a heavy weight was pressing on them.

We often exaggerate the burdens when we picture ourselves as holding up the church as the Greeks used to picture Atlas holding up the world. We never stand alone in holding up the church, even if we think we do. But church life does include heavy burdens. One of the most frustrating aspects is that they offer no relief. Problems come from every side, often with little warning. They may include tensions over honest differences of opinion. They may involve assisting in the personal problems of dear friends. The experiences leave us exhausted, knowing that we cannot simply walk away. Thus, the burdens of church life are often increased because we see no end to our struggle and no retirement from service. This is often disillusioning to those who expect the Christian life to be a release from burdens.

According to 2 Corinthians, the true disciple is not disillusioned by the disappointments of service. He understands that these burdens are a part of the total "job description" of the servant of Christ. When Paul was challenged to prove that he was "of Christ" (10:7), or "a Christian," he told of his labors. He experienced "no rest" for his spirit (2:13); a troublesome church had given him sleepless nights. He experienced grief caused by rebellious people (2:1-4). In addition, he experienced the problem of going on in the presence of ill health (12:7), exhaustion, and persecution. In one particularly vivid statement, Paul tells of persecution so severe that he was "utterly, unbearably crushed" and "despaired of life itself" (1:8). It was as if a weight were about to crush him. Paul's ministry had brought nothing but burdens. No end to the struggle seemed to be in view.

The opening section of 2 Corinthians (1:3-11) is filled with this theme. Paul customarily opens his letters with a thanksgiving which includes references to the major subjects of the book (cf. Romans 1:8-17; 1 Corinthians 1:4). The "thanksgiving" section of 2 Corinthians refers to affliction, a theme which is pursued throughout the book (1:4, 6, 8; 2:4; 4:17; 6:4; 7:4; 8:2, 13). A reference to the sufferings of Christians is also made (1:5, 6). In addition, he mentions a time when he thought that he had received the "sentence of death" (1:9). We do not know any details about this incident, for Paul includes it here only to remind us of the burdens involved in being Christ's servant. He sets the tone of the Epistles by drawing our attention to the various burdens of the Christian life.

Why must the service to Christ be "crushing"? In 1:5, Paul seems to assume that his readers understand. "For as we share abundantly in Christ's sufferings" suggests a basic fact about the Christian life: Jesus did not "bear the cross alone." The NEB renders the verse appropriately: "As Christ's cup of sufferings overflows, and we suffer with him. . . ." The "sufferings of Christ" did not end with the crucifixion. They extended into the life of His people. Jesus had once told His disciples that they would have to "take up the cross" in order to follow Him (Mark 8:34). On numerous occasions, Paul speaks in graphic terms of the "fellowship" (or "participation") in Christ's sufferings (Philippians 3:10). To the Galatians, he wrote, ". . . I bear on my body the marks of Jesus" (Galatians 6:17). To the Colossians, he wrote, ". . . I complete what is lacking in Christ's afflictions" (Colossians 1:24). The service to Christ is burdensome, therefore, because Christ's sufferings continue in the church. When we are burdened by the pain of others, we are participating in the suffering which Christ began.

Those of us who find the burdens of church life disillusioning can find a healthy realism in Paul's acceptance of anguish for the sake of Christ. The burdens of his activity are never described as unfortunate interruptions in a blissful Christian life. The oppressive weight of the "anxiety for all the churches" (11:28) was a necessary part of the Christian life which contained exhausting burdens. This fact causes us to ask, Where is the good news about the Christian life?

THE GOD OF ALL COMFORT (1:3)

The remarkable fact about Paul's references to the afflictions and burdens of the Christian life is that he recalls these moments of desperation in 1:3-11 in the context of a thanksgiving! He did not recall these moments to inform us that Christianity can be burdensome, for he begins the section with words of praise: "Blessed be the God and Father of our Lord Jesus Christ, the Father of mercies and God of all comfort." The emphasis is on God's power and mercy. "Blessed be the God," which is used in two other instances in the New Testament at the beginning of a letter (Ephesians 1:3; 1 Peter 1:3), is a traditional Jewish way of responding in gratitude to God (cf. 11:31; Luke 1:68; Romans 1:25; 9:5). Just as Job responded to pain with the words, ". . . Blessed be the name of the Lord" (Job 1:21), Paul opens his account of his burdens with words of thanksgiving.

If we wonder how Paul was capable of enduring the burdens which his faith brought him, the answer is found in his view of God, who is the "God of all comfort" (1:3). The word "comfort" appears more often in 2 Corinthians than in all of Paul's other epistles combined. In 1:3-8, the word appears no less then ten times. It is no accident that the words about divine comfort appear most often in the one letter where Paul speaks in the most detail about his afflictions for Christ's sake. Paul can withstand affliction because God "comforts us in all our affliction" (1:4). His burdens were never carried alone.

An old theme of the Bible is that God "comforts us in all our affliction." The Bible never suggests that faith involves the absence of pain. When Paul became a Christian, the Lord said to Ananias, "I will show him how much he must suffer for the sake of my name" (Acts 9:16). In the Old Testament, the people of God often experienced the desolation which made them fear that God was absent or in hiding. There was a moment when Israel had been defeated, and her cities were left in ruins." . . . She has none to comfort her. . . . She has no comforter" (Lamentations 1:2, 9). She says, "For these things I weep; my eyes flow with tears; for a comforter is far from me, one to revive my courage; . . . " (Lamentations 1:16).

In a tragic moment, only God Himself can bring comfort. The psalmist says, "thy rod and Thy staff, they comfort me" (Psalms 23:4). In one of the most beautiful passages of Scripture, God speaks to His desolate people, saying, "Comfort, comfort my people, says your God. Speak tenderly to Jerusalem, and cry to her that her warfare is ended, that her iniquity is pardoned, that she has received from the Lord's hand double for all her sins" (Isaiah 40:1, 2).

When Isaiah surveys a desolate people, he anticipates the day when one comes to "comfort all who mourn" (Isaiah 61:2). When Paul describes God as the "God of all comfort," he is recalling the history of his people. God had not prevented pain, but He had been the God of comfort.

The word "comfort" has been so weakened and cheapened that we are likely to miss the triumphant spirit of Paul's description of God as the one "who comforts us in all our affliction." Comfort may suggest to us our attempts to say a consoling word to one who is grieving. We speak also of a "comfortable income" and a "comfortable home." In the Bible, "comfort" is far more than a kind word or a perfect tranquilizer. God's comfort is His power to strengthen and save.

This meaning is suggested when the prophet addresses a despairing people with the words, "O afflicted one, storm-tossed, and not comforted, . . ." (Isaiah 54:11). Then he says, "I have seen his ways, but I will heal him; I will lead him and requite him with comfort, . . ." (Isaiah 57:18). God's comfort, therefore, is His power to rescue and heal.

A VIVID MEMORY (1:8-11)

Paul has a vivid memory of a moment when God came to his aid. It was when he experienced affliction in Asia (1:8). He was "utterly, unbearably crushed," and he "despaired of life itself." Paul's word for "crushed" means literally "weighed down." The image suggests a cargo ship that has been overloaded. The "despair" indicated his recognition that he could not calculate a way out of his dilemma. On his own resources, no solution could be found. All of the burdens of ministry were overloading his capacities to carry them. He had in mind both the physical and emotional ordeals of ministry: sickness, pain, and the anxiety for the churches (cf. 5:4; 11:28). There was no way that he could carry the load. It was sure to crush him.

That experience gave Paul the perspective which led him to describe God as the One "who comforts us in all our affliction" (1:4). Paul had previously failed to calculate the strengthening presence of God. But in the moment of despair, Paul learned to rely on God's resurrection power, and not on himself (1:9). God's comfort was not limited to kind words. It was the power which rescued him from a deadly peril and gave him the strength to continue his ministry. From that momemt on, Paul discovered that "he will deliver us again" (1:10).

Authentic Christianity consists in our opening ourselves to various troubles for the sake of God's cause. But, as Paul reminds us, we do not rely on ourselves. Our faith tells about one who comes to our side when we believe that we are "utterly, unbearably crushed." As Paul says later, ". . . when I am weak, then I am strong" (12:10).

Our ministries often fail because we have been unwilling to have a faith similar to Paul's in the one who "comforts us in all our affliction." In some instances, we have conducted our ministries by our own resources and ingenuity, leaving no place for God's comforting power. Authentic ministry experiences both the burdens and the divine comfort. The absence of either of these will make our work ineffective.

SHARING COMFORT WITH OTHERS (1:4-7)

God's comfort comes in many ways. It came to Paul in his deliverance from a desperate situation. But God's comfort comes also through other people. Indeed, Paul's major point at the opening of 2 Corinthians (1:3-7) is that he has become the agent of God's comforting presence. He has been comforted by God for the very purpose of comforting others: "So that we may be able to comfort those who are in any affliction" (1:4). He knows that he is not the only one who has been desperate; others share "the same sufferings" (1:6) as he has suffered—emotional, physical, and spiritual. Surely others would benefit from a sharing of the strength which he has received from God. They could find it easier to endure their own trials if another was there to pass on the comfort which he has already received.

Paul knew that God had a purpose for his recent trials. He was to comfort others with the comfort which he had received (1:4). In a striking expression in 1:5, Paul describes the "over-flowing" (NIV) of both Christ's sufferings and his comfort. The image of "overflowing" suggests that the church is a community where "no man is an island." Our burdens overflow from one to another. In the same way, there is a "sharing" (1:7) and an "overflowing" of comfort. If we stood alone with our burdens, we might easily be crushed. But we are strengthened by others in the church whose past experience gives us hope.

Our ministries fail if we allow our private experience of frustration and anxiety to preoccupy our minds. God's comfort comes to us through others. If we, like Paul, have discovered God's power at a time of weakness, this news is to be shared. If we see ourselves "crushed," we need those who can share with us the comfort which they have received from God. The burden of one may finally serve a useful purpose to the whole community. As Paul said, "If we are afflicted, it is for your comfort and salvation" (1:6).

ANOTHER PERSONAL EXPERIENCE (7:5-16)

Paul was not only the source of comfort to others; sometimes he needed the comfort which only another Christian could provide. There was the time when he was "afflicted at every turn—fighting without and fear within" (7:5). The situation of a troubled church had apparently left him with sleepless nights and severe emotional exhaustion: "But my mind could not rest because I did not find my brother Titus there [in Troas]" (2:13). A troublesome church had left Paul exhausted. Its history of discontent and rebellion had made it appear that his labors would result in nothing.

Church troubles are not new. Behind Paul's own struggle was the open rebellion at Corinth which had brought him considerable grief (2:5). The persistent troubles at Corinth had left him in despair. He had not given up, for he held out hope that Titus might bring him good news from the Corinthians.

The news from Titus was a source of extraordinary joy. The Corinthians has been grieved into repenting (7:6).Their grief had not resulted in hostility and abandonment of the faith, for it had been "godly grief" (7:10). Paul does not often speak of the repentence of Christians. This passage is a rare reminder of

Paul's conviction that our failures can lead us to the "godly grief" which produces repentance. Those who are the source of immense difficulty can change.

The coming of Titus was the source of new comfort for Paul: "But God, who comforts the downcast, comforted us by the coming of Titus" (7:6). This incident is an example of the way in which God's people mediate comfort to each other. Paul is comforted when Titus is comforted by the Corinthians' change of heart. The Corinthians are able to comfort Titus, who is able to comfort Paul. The passage resounds with relief and joy. There is more to the Christian life than heavy burdens. "I rejoice," says Paul, ". . . because you were grieved into repenting" (7:9). He speaks of the joy of Titus, whose mind has also been set to rest (7:13).

He concludes the section with the words, "I rejoice, because I have perfect confidence in you" (7:16). The anxiety over troubled churches may lead to the hopeless feeling that church life involves one painful struggle after another. But church life involves infinitely more. The ties of affection provide memories of joy and strength. These ties are often strong enough to make us forget the unpleasant moments. Titus reported the "longing," "mourning," and "zeal" of the Corinthians for Paul (7:7). While the unpleasant aspects of the past were forgotten, they would never forget that their Christian commitment had produced the kind of affection that came from being fellow strugglers. Even Titus, who had known the Corinthians briefly, was moved by the new bonds of fellowship. Paul says, "And his heart goes out all the more to you, as he remembers the obedience of you all, and the fear and trembling with which you received him" (7:15).

CONCLUSION

If my experience is at all like that of most active Christians, we may conclude that an active commitment to Christ will lead us into tense moments of disagreement, periods when leaders are subject to constant criticism, and times of honest disagreements with other Christians and my work with others resulting in disappointment. But fellow Christians were always a source of courage. Some of those whom we had tried to encourage finally encouraged us! If Paul could see nothing less than God's comfort in the coming of Titus, undoubtedly, we can see God at work in those who bring us good news.

God may not offer a tranquilizer to remove from us the anxiety of ministry, but He sends comfort to us in many ways. He sends it through good friends, good news, and the strength which prevents us from giving in to despair.

8

CAPTIVES OF GOD'S LOVE
(5:11-21)

"So we are ambassadors for Christ, ..." (5:20).

The Corinthians had heard the words before: "One has died for all" (5:14). In fact, words almost identical to these were among the first words that the Corinthians had ever heard about Jesus Christ (cf. 1 Corinthians 15:3). On Paul's first visit to Corinth, that simple message had brought them to obey Jesus Christ. Wherever Paul had gone on his missionary journeys, the content of his message was always the same: "One has died for all," or "Christ died for our sins." The Christian story could be summarized in those words.

If the Corinthians had heard these words many times before, we must ask why Paul bothers to return to this summary in 5:14. Paul has been in the middle of his defense of his work. The entire section, 2:14—7:4, is composed of Paul's defense against critics who say that he is not a true servant of Christ. Then suddenly, in 5:14, Paul throws in the words which every Christian must know by heart: "One has died for all." But he does not stop with reminding the Corinthians of his message. He proceeds in 5:12-19 to summarize the message in new words. The words of 5:19, "In Christ God was reconciling the world to himself," may be the most powerful statement of the Christian story anywhere in the New Testament. Perhaps the Corinthians knew these words by heart also. They ring with such power that we can imagine congregations repeating them regularly in worship. We can imagine Christians, upon being asked to summarize what they believe, saying, "In Christ God was reconciling the world to himself," or "Christ died for our sins." Perhaps they would have replied with the words of 5:21: "For our sake he made him to be sin who knew no sin, so that in him we might become the righteousness of God." The impression we get is that others are wanting to debate who the true Christians are, and Paul flings back his heaviest ammunition.

SO THAT YOU MAY ANSWER (5:11, 12)

What do those summaries of the faith have to do with the question, "Who is a true Christian?" The Corinthians were bewildered because others had come with their own idea of what the Christian faith was. Indeed, they were left not knowing what to believe after they heard the counterclaims of those claiming to be the true servants of Christ. Some "compare themselves" against others (10:12) and judge others by their outward appearance (5:12). Apparently, they claimed to have the gift of the Spirit, arguing that true servants of Christ could be identified by visible manifestations of power. Such an unimpressive man as Paul could not possibly have the Spirit, for he has no power to display! Paul has to defend himself against the charge that he is a "worldly" or "unspiritual" man (1:17; 5:16; 10:3, 4).

Paul does not defend himself against his critics for the sake of his own honor. He sees that the Corinthians would easily lose their direction if they are not given some answers. The entire church needs to understand and be informed. ". . . what we are is known to God," says Paul, "and I hope it is known also to your conscience" (5:11). Then he adds, "We are not commending ourselves to you again but giving you cause to be proud of us, so that you may be able to answer those who pride themselves on a man's position and not on his heart" (5:12). An uninformed church would be defenseless against competing versions of the Christian faith! Without answers, the Christian does not know what the mark of the Christian is.

The word which is translated "answer" in the RSV (*aphorme*) was a military word for the basis of operations in a military campaign. At times, the words was used for the resources necessary for a campaign. The success or failure of a military campaign depends on adequate resources and supply lines. For Paul, the church also is left defenseless without provisions for the campaign. In our case, the provisions are answers, the essentials of the faith. Paul was saying, "How can I talk about my work as God's servant without returning to the most fundamental principles of all? If we lose these, we have lost everything!"

No greater model for solving serious questions in the church exists than the one which Paul offers. Although the Corinthian church had heard many times the words, "One has died for all," they needed to hear the essential message again. Paul's method for answering a disputed point may seem strange to us. We are practical people, and we may be more interested in what will "work" or achieve results than in what is "true." Furthermore, we love new ideas so much that we easily decide that the old message is worn out and not worthy of repeating. But Paul brings out the old message at a critical moment because it is the only standard for determining what the mark of the Christian is. Our provision for the battle is the story of the One who died for all.

Richard Neuhaus wrote in *Freedom for Ministry* that "among the 3,000 and more local churches in America, almost anything in the line of ministry can be found."[1] With all of the different styles of ministry, it is obvious that some programs are worthwhile for God's people and some are not. When church leaders look at the many alternative programs, how do they determine which ones actually serve the cause of Christ? Is there a way for determining whether to initiate a family life program, construct a new facility, or counsel troubled people? The church without resources in the basic story has no direction.

---

[1]Richard John Neuhaus, *Freedom for Ministry* (New York: Harper & Row, 1979), 35.

THE STORY IS OUR STORY (5:13-15)

The mark of the Christian is not only in saying the right words, for even the right words can become meaningless phrases. In 5:13, 14, Paul shows that the words, "One has died for all," were not meaningless to him. When he wanted to explain why his work did not satisfy those who considered him unimpressive by outward appearance, he recalled the impact of the words, "One has died for all," on his life. We get an impression of the principles which determined Paul's work when he says, "For if we are beside ourselves, it is for God; if we are in our right mind, it is for you" (5:13). Perhaps Paul stated the basic principles by which he worked because others had said that he was in his "right mind" (the KJV has "sober"), and not "ecstatic" enough. The word for "beside ourselves" is literally "ecstatic" (*exestemen*). Paul answers, "If I am ecstatic, this ecstasy is between God and me. I do not parade my achievements before others to advance myself." Paul does not "look out for number one." His ministry, according to 5:13, is "for God" and for others. The mark of God's servant is his rejection of selfishness and egoism.

What could make Paul reject the standard of his culture and ours? He answers in 5:14: "For the love of Christ controls us." The word "controls" (*synechei*) is striking. It meant "take into custody" or "impel." It was the word for the prisoner who has been held in custody by a superior power. Paul has "been captured" and "held in custody" by the love of Christ. He looks and acts differently from others because he has been overwhelmed by his love. He acts out of selfless love because love now controls him.

Paul speaks elsewhere of this overwhelming love: "God shows his love for us in that while we were yet sinners Christ died for us" (Romans 5:8). "Who shall separate us from the love of Christ?" he asks (Romans 8:35). He was personally moved that he had been loved. That fact shaped his ministry.

When Paul recalled the love which controlled him, he thought of the cross. Now we understand why. In a discussion over true and false servants of God, he quotes the old words, "One has died for all." The phrase was not a meaningless cliché.

He recalled each day that Christianity began with an act of selfless love when Jesus Christ rejected the standard of self-centeredness. At the center of the faith is the simple word "for." He died "for" our sins (1 Corinthians 15:3) and "for the ungodly" (Romans 5:6).

If Jesus was the selfless one, what is the mark of the Christian? Paul answers, ". . . one has died for all; therefore all have died. And he died for all, that those who live might live no longer for themselves but for him who for their sake died and was raised" (5:14, 15). The mark of the Christian is that he is no longer preoccupied with his own achievements, reputation, or fame. Those who belong to Christ are distinguished by their willingness to live for others.

If we "overhear" Paul's conversation with the Corinthians, we will raise new questions about the way we determine our priorities. How often do we return to the basic words, "One has died for all," to discover our direction? Do we choose leaders whose distinction is that they "no longer live for themselves"? We, like the Corinthians, are tempted by approaches which have an impressive appearance. For some, the mark of the authentic church is visible success. We may choose ministries which will "put us on the map." If, however, we continue to return to Jesus' example to find our direction, we will be "taken captive" by His way. Verner Eller has correctly said that Christ calls us, not to be successful, but to be faithful.[2]

GOD'S NEW WORLD (5:16, 17)

The possibility always exists that we can go on repeating the central statements of our faith week after week without recognizing that they have an impact on our lives. I recall one evening worship service where the minister's sermon was interrupted by a voice from the audience which said, "So what?" The question, embarrassing for both the minister and the audience, was inappropriate for its setting. But the incident

---

[2]Verner Eller, *Outward Bound* (Grand Rapids, Mich.: Wm. B. Eerdmans Publishing Co., 1930), 47.

reminded me that there is a "So what?" to the old story, for it makes a difference in our lives. Our ministries can go on with "business as usual," unaffected by the story of the cross. Paul's "therefore" in 5:16, 17 shows that he was not satisfied to repeat that "one has died for all." That story has made a difference in his ministry, as the two parallel sentences show in 5:16, 17.

The point of 5:16, 17 is that the crucifixion—that event which was foolish by human standards—has given Paul a totally new way of looking at the world. "From now on" refers to the new experience in Christ that has changed him. No longer does he "regard" (or "know") anyone from a "human point of view" (*kata sarka*; NEB, "by worldly standards"). The cross means the end of worldly standards, for there is an entirely new way of looking at the world and at Jesus Christ. This point is brought out forcefully in 5:17. The NEB translates 5:17, "When anyone is united in Christ, there is a whole new world." It is true, as the RSV renders the passage, that one who has been united to Christ "is a new creation." But the Greek can as easily be rendered, "There is a new world" for the Christian, since the Christian sees the world in a new way. Standards which once were important have ceased to be priority items. Values which once meant nothing have suddenly become meaningful. This change of values have grown out of the story of a defenseless man who died on a cross. Because that story means something to me, "from now on" I shall evaluate ministries according to God's standards.

Paul's new "point of view" in Christ raises critical issues in the life of the church today. In a time when we remain uncertain in determining which ministries have priority, it is appropriate for us to ask if our programs reflect the "human point of view" of Paul's opponents or the "new world" of the cross. And what determines a successful ministry? By the "human point of view," Paul "wasted his time" on several "unproductive" ministries. Is it appropriate to evaluate all ministries by the "numbers" principle, as if we could measure our success by some kind of "scorekeeping"? By the "new world" point of view, success will never be measured by some kind of quantitative score, as in the schools, or by the standing in the profit and loss column, as in the corporation.

I am convinced that many important programs which conform to the new "point of view" are never publicized. They are often carried on in difficult circumstances where the results are unimpressive. But they are carried on by people who have devoted themselves to others. I recall missionaries who worked for decades in unreceptive fields and families who refused to give up on the church in a changing neighborhood. Many of these people had no impressive statistics to demonstrate their effectiveness. Those who measured them by the human standards saw only failure. But these people refused to get caught up in the "human point of view" as a measure of success.

WHOSE MINISTRY IS IT? (5:18-21)

Our natural egos tempt us to live by the "human point of view." We are tempted to look for programs which advance *us* and give us reason to take pride in our achievements. We are also tempted to avoid legitimate ministries which do not have a great potential for success. There is natural ego at stake when our desire is to have the "greatest" church or to minister to the "most prestigious" church. There is a time to raise the question, especially when we are caught up with our own egos: Whose ministry is it?

Paul answers this question in 5:18, 19. The emphasis is on the fact that "all this is from God." In verses 18 and 19, he summarizes the Christian story, as he did in 5:14, in order to remind us that this is "from God." In two parallel sentences he says that God "reconciled us to himself" through Christ (5:18) and in Christ (5:19). That is, the story began with God's initiative. We did nothing to restore ourselves to Him.

When Paul told the story of the cross, he used a striking image to declare what God had done, an image which Paul rarely uses. At the cross God "reconciled" us to Himself. The word implies the restoration of peace and harmony after a period of estrangement (cf. 1 Corinthians 7:11). The word reminds us of the Hebrew greeting, *shalom*, which was commonly given as a greeting on the street. The word meant "peace," but it meant more than the absence of hostility. It implied the experience of harmony and wholeness. God acted through Christ to do what our initiatives could not have done: He restored us to *shalom*. As Paul says in Romans 5:1, "We have peace with God through our Lord Jesus Christ." After being "enemies," we were "reconciled to God by the death of his Son" (Romans 5:10). It was a different way of saying what had been said earlier (5:14): "One has died for all." It is God's story, not ours.

But how are others to know the story? In 5:18-20, each time Paul summarizes the story ("God was reconciling us"), he also mentions those to whom God has entrusted the story. If God has reconciled us, we take a "ministry of reconciliation" (5:18). Our ministry is, according to 5:18, a *gift* ("gave us the ministry of reconciliation"). According to 5:19, it is a "trust." It is not our ministry, to do as we wish. The programs are not our programs. Legitimate programs never compete with each other. Indeed, every genuine ministry is intended to be a "ministry of reconciliation."

While modern ministries often fail because they lack direction and definition, Paul lacked no such direction. His ministry, as a "ministry of reconciliation," lacked no definition. Every deed and every aspect of his ministry was directed toward bringing *shalom*, or reconciliation, between God and man. He is the "ambassador" of Christ (5:20). The word "ambassador" was a very dignified word, unlike some other terms for ministry (i.e., "slave," 4:5; "servant," 6:4). In Paul's day, as in our own, the ambassador had the right to speak fully for his leader. Those to whom he spoke knew that his words were actually the words of his sovereign. When he worked for peace, behind him stood the full authority of the emperor. Thus, when Paul appeals to others to accept God's "peace," it is God who appeals through the minister.

CONCLUSION

The words of Paul, spoken at a time when the focus of the church's ministry was much debated, must be heard today.

Wherever we look for direction and purpose for our programs, we dare not overlook the essential fact that God's "word of reconciliation" has been entrusted to His servants. The church has lost its way when it has forgotten that it exists to say to others, "Be reconciled to God." A "true church" returns repeatedly to the one simple story which called her to life: "One has died for all, therefore all have died." If we speak and act only from a "human point of view," we lose our reason for existing. Indeed, we may be successful from a "human point of view" and lose our way. There is an urgent summons in every generation to ask: Is our ministry a reflection of God's "new world" of values?

9

AN HONORABLE REPUTATION
(8:1—9:15)

"We intend that no one should blame us about this liberal gift. . . ." (8:20).

In the life of the local congregation today, any discussion of the church's finances is likely to receive one of two possible responses. In one response, we are likely to hear resentment over what seems to be the church's incessant requests for money. The other response expresses more boredom than resentment. Any public discussion of the budget is, according to this view, a thing to be avoided and an unnecessary intrusion into the more important concerns of the church. Behind both reactions to any discussion of the church's finances is an unspoken assumption: The financial commitments of the church are, at best, a harmless diversion for those who are interested in such unspiritual matters as money and budgets. According to this view, money and budgets have little to do with the ministry of the church.

Second Corinthians, the epistle primarily devoted to the defense of Paul's ministry, contains two chapters on the collection. The collection was apparently one of the most important commitments of Paul's entire ministry. Early in his ministry, he had committed himself to the collection of funds for the poor among the Christians of Jerusalem (Galatians 2:10). He then mentioned the collection briefly in his first letter to the Corinthians (16:1, 2). When he later wrote the letter to the

Romans at a turning point in his life (Romans 15:22-29), several years had passed, and the collection had not yet been delivered to Jerusalem. But Paul had not given up on delivering it, for this was one of the major projects of his life. He was willing to risk his personal safety in bringing the collection to Jerusalem.

Since the collection took Paul a period of several years to assemble, he was interested, evidently, in more than mere famine relief. The money, coming from the Gentile churches, for the benefit of the Jewish churches, was to symbolize the unity of the church. It symbolized sacrifice, love, and the priorities of the churches. Paul was in no sense hesitant to talk about money, for he knew that money represents us—our labor and our love. The way we spend our money indicates what things in life are important to us. If Gentile churches could sacrifice for the home churches of Jerusalem, they would be sending a clear message of concern for their welfare.

A strong appeal for financial support is especially remarkable in 2 Corinthians, for a major part of the book suggests that Paul's integrity has been questioned. Some had considered it suspicious that Paul had accepted no money from the Corinthians (11:7-11) for his work. He himself had chosen to be in want and to depend on other churches rather than burden the Corinthians (11:9). Nevertheless, a time came for him to speak of money. A year had passed since he had made his first appeal (8:10). He makes his appeal in chapters 8 and 9, not for himself, but for the great project of his life. Perhaps he now turns to the subject because he is convinced that trust is sufficiently restored for him to ask the Corinthians for money. The collections, the distribution, and the record-keeping—those items we often consider boring and unnecessary—were necessary for his ministry.

A MODEL CHURCH (8:1-6)

We often benefit from having appropriate models. Individual Christians sometimes serve as models of Christian ministry and provide an insight into the meaning of service. In the same way, a whole congregation can offer a challenge of authentic service. It can show us what ministries are possible for us and stimulate us to better service. In 8:1-6, the Macedonian church is a model of generosity (8:2) for the Corinthians (cf. Romans 15:26). They, like every other church, had experienced a "test of affliction" (cf. 1:7; 1 Thessalonians 1:6; 2:14). What distinguished the Macedonians was that they passed the test in a remarkable way.

The Macedonian church also provides an appropriate model for the contemporary congregation. We are most impressed by the intensity of their commitment in which their "extreme poverty" overflowed "in a wealth of liberality on their part" (8:2). They gave "beyond their means" (8:3). We who wonder how to motivate an affluent church to give liberally are naturally amazed at a congregation which gives liberally out of its great poverty. The Macedonian Christians' poverty, some have suggested, was a result of their Christian commitment. In an area that was reasonably prosperous, they were poor. Probably some had lost their jobs and source of income because of their Christian commitment. Nevertheless, they gave liberally.

Paul's word for "liberality" (*haplotes*, 8:2) meant literally "singleness." The word suggests the "singleness of heart" of one who has no mixed motives (cf. Colossians 3:22; Ephesians 6:5). When it is used for the giving of money, it suggests the "liberality" of one who recognizes only one priority (cf. Romans 12:8). The word indicates why the Macedonians could give liberally from their great poverty: their "singleness of heart" meant that they were not divided in their priorities. Their commitments were not divided between the work of the church and other pursuits. The giving of their money reflected the priority of their lives. The Macedonians are thus a model for us and a reminder that liberal giving grows out of the single-minded pursuit of a goal. Those whose attention is divided between the desire to keep up with every new material advantage and their commitment to the cause of Christ will find it impossible to give liberally, despite their relative affluence. Those who are "single-minded" give out of their poverty.

I suspect that our failure to give enthusiastically results from the fact that we speak of budgets, programs, bonded indebtedness, and financial obligations in the same way that we might describe any financial venture. This language leads us to think of the finances of the church as "unspiritual" matters. We can learn a valuable lesson from the early church on this, for the early Christians never used ordinary fiscal language to describe their giving. It is particularly impressive that the Macedonians begged for the "favor of taking part in the relief of the saints" (8:4). The NIV renders the passage, "the privilege of sharing in this service to the saints." The collection was not a mere financial obligation; it involved a "service to the saints." The Greek word translated "relief" (RSV) or "service" (NIV; NEB) is *diakonia*, which is the usual word for "ministry" in the New Testament.

"Ministry" (*diakonia*) was an important word in the New Testament. Originally, the word referred to an act of self-abasement: waiting at table and serving food. It involved living for others as a household servant lived for his master. Jesus gave the word dignity by coming as a servant of others (Matthew 20:28) and by demanding that His disciples serve each other (Luke 22:26). The mark of His disciples was to be *diakonia*, the selfless ministry of building up one another. Ministry is the loving service to others (cf. 1 Corinthians 16:15; Hebrews 6:10; Philemon 13; 2 Timothy 1:18).

There are, according to the New Testament, many ways to minister. The "work of ministry" is the task of the whole church (Ephesians 4:12). "There are varieties of service," says Paul, "but the same Lord" (1 Corinthians 12:5). One important ministry is the contribution of money. When the Macedonians wanted to take part in aiding the Jerusalem church, they saw here a ministry that would build up the church. When Paul took the collection to Jerusalem, he went to serve the saints (Romans 15:25). There are many forms of ministry in which we show that we no longer live for ourselves (5:15). The contribution should be one way among many that we demonstrate that we have, like the Macedonians, given ourselves to the Lord (8:5).

If we are "ministering" when we share in the contribution, there is a reason for the church not to lose sight of the fact that all ministries are meant to serve others in some way. We do not contribute merely in order to set new records or to create monuments to ourselves. Every ministry is intended to continue the work of the One who gave Himself for others. Many of us recognize that our essential ministries begin with our commitment to "give ourselves": for the special contribution for disaster relief, for the supplies and staff to teach our children, and for the work of the missionary. We have the possibility, as did the Macedonians, not only of sharing in programs, committees, and budget reports, but also of sharing in exciting ministries.

A PROOF OF LOVE (8:7-15)

The Macedonians had passed their test (cf. 8:2) by demonstrating that they had given themselves to the Lord (8:5). Paul now turns to the Corinthians to give the "proof" of their love (8:7, 8). As the NIV reads, "I want to test the sincerity of your love by comparing it with the earnestness of others." It is never enough just to claim deep devotion and affection, for love is always tested in our willingness to sacrifice for others. It can become hypocritical (Romans 12:9). Paul had already shown his love for the Corinthians in his many visits, letters, and even sleepless nights (cf. 2:4; 6:6). Christ had demonstrated His love by giving up His wealth "for our sake" in order to make us rich (8:9). Genuine love has always been visible in real deeds of serving others. Consequently, Paul says, "So give proof, before the churches, of your love and of our boasting about you to these men" (8:24). It is good for a church to have a good model for ministry, as the Corinthians had one in the Macedonians. But there is a time for *becoming a model* by giving a demonstration that our love is not hypocritical.

When we read Paul's challenge to the Corinthians, we can identify with them. Most of us have not, like the Macedonians, "passed the test" by emptying ourselves for others in loving service. The Corinthians, in the midst of their many debates, were being challenged to prove that they remembered the church's purpose. Throughout the centuries, there have been few great churches who have remembered that their task was to follow Jesus' example of "becoming poor" for the sake of others. Churches, like individuals, are tempted to "make a name for themselves" and exercise power and influence. The church sometimes resembles a social club which exists only to entertain and provide a convenient place for its own people. We, like the Corinthians, face the test that many churches have failed. We pass the test when we repeat in our congregational life the loving service toward others that Jesus demonstrated when he "became poor" for our sakes.

TO AVOID ANY CRITICISM (8:17-24)

Those who ask for contributions come naturally under the suspicion that they are exploiting the sacrificial giving of others in order to enrich themselves. This suspicion is often reinforced by scandals involving religious organizations. The media commonly report on religious tax-exempt organizations who use the most sophisticated equipment to raise funds. Then a major part of that income is used to raise more funds. In many instances, it appears that the organization exists for no other purpose than to raise funds. More is spent in raising funds than in any act of service.

The legitimate ministry cannot avoid suspicion of hucksterism. Paul is fully aware of the suspicions which this "liberal gift" (8:20) would arouse. How could the casual observer, to say nothing of someone who has already questioned his integrity, be sure that Paul's ministry was legitimate? He appears to take no chances on a question as important as his integrity in handling money. He does not handle the money alone. He sends Titus, whose commitment has already been shown in difficult circumstances (7:5-16), to the Corinthians. Titus is accompanied by one who is identified only as "the brother who is famous among all the churches" (8:18) for his preaching. The reliability of the brother is indicated by the fact that he was specifically appointed by churches who placed their trust in him. A third companion is identified simply as "our brother" (8:22). He, too, has "been tested and found earnest." All of these men are "messengers of the churches" (8:23), men whose integrity has never been questioned.

In 8:20, 21, Paul tells why he took elaborate precautions in handling the church's money. The NIV renders his words, "We want to avoid any criticism of the way we administer this liberal gift" (8:20). Paul knew that it was not enough for the authentic minister to act with integrity; he must leave no doubt about his integrity (cf. 8:21). In similar language, he had said in 6:3, ". . . so that no fault may be found with our ministry." In 8:19, 20, Paul recognizes that his ministry involves the handling of money. Indeed, the verb *diakoneo* ("minister") is used in both verses, where it is rendered "administer" by the NIV. The whole church may take part in a ministry, but some have the ministry of collecting and distributing the funds.

The church needs to recognize the validity of Paul's statement that "we aim at what is honorable not only in the Lord's sight but also in the sight of men" (8:21; cf. Proverbs 3:4). We who urge others to "give themselves" by generous contributions have the responsibility of removing all doubts about the integrity of those who handle money and the efficiency of our methods of collecting and distributing it. A church which has a reputation for handling funds in an irresponsible way will create the cynicism that destroys the spirit of generous giving. A church which has a record for spending the money of others in a reckless way will also destroy the desire to be involved in the ministry of giving. There is a legitimate ministry, therefore, for those who are capable of keeping records, improving the church's accounting procedures, and informing others how the money is spent. We overlook an important aspect of our faith when we separate the church's work into the spiritual and the material sides. Paul saw himself as a "minister" in handling funds. A legitimate ministry avoids the carelessness that could lead to doubts about its prudence and honesty.

THIS PUBLIC SERVICE (9:1-12)

A ministry which fails after an enthusiastic beginning can demoralize us. Such a failure may be caused by circumstances and issues which seem more urgent to us than the ministry we have planned. The Corinthians' role in the collection is an example of the way in which legitimate ministries can be ignored for a while. On two instances, Paul reminds his readers that their special ministry remains uncompleted after a year's wait (8:10; 9:2). He reminds them that it is not enough to have great plans; the great task is to execute the plans that have been made. He says "so that your readiness in desiring it may be matched by your completing it out of what you have" (8:11). Many churches have made bold plans, but few have followed through to completion.

It is easier to dream about new projects than to maintain the commitment to old ones. When we explain new ones, we find it is easier to describe in glowing terms what is possible. But when we summon the commitment for an old ministry, we must say with Paul, "Now it is superfluous for me to write to you about the offering for the saints" (9:1). The verse can be rendered, "It is superflous *to go on writing* to you. . . ." The ministry (*diakonia*, 9:1) has been explained before; nothing is new in it.

How do we maintain a ministry that has lost its novelty? I suspect that, as Paul writes to the Corinthians, he fears that they will embarrass him before the other churches. After a year, there is now a special urgency in the project (9:4). He begins to encourage them by reminding them that the collection is a "ministry" or "service" (9:1). Then he proceeds to tell the Corinthians that their past commitment to this ministry had already "stirred up" the Macedonians. The Macedonian church, this great model of sacrificial ministry (8:1-7), was originally "stirred up" by the example of the Corinthians themselves (9:1-5)! Churches learn from each other. At different times in a congregation's life, it may alternate between being a good example and following a good example. From the moment when Jesus provided us with the example of service as a way of life, we have learned from each other.

Ministries are enhanced by a good memory. The memory

can remind us of the good influence we once had. We recall that our example encouraged others. It would be demoralizing, therefore, to give up on a ministry in which we once provided leadership.

The Macedonians are now the model for the Corinthians. In 8:2, Paul had described their extraordinary liberality. The same word, meaning "singleness of purpose" (*haplotes*), is now employed in the appeals to the Corinthians in 9:11, 13, where it is translated "generosity." It is as if Paul had said, "It is time for you to show the same single-minded commitment to service which the Macedonians showed." Their participation in this act of service was a way of sending signals everywhere that their priorities were firmly established. The emphasis on giving with a cheerful heart (9:7) reminds us of the joy in the life of the man who sold all that he had to buy the field in Jesus' parable (Matthew 13:44). We "give sparingly" (9:6) when our priorities have not been established. When we are single-minded, we can be cheerful givers (9:7).

Nothing evokes a generous response as clearly as the recognition that our sacrifice has a good purpose. Paul's terminology in referring to the collection leaves no doubt about its real purpose. In 9:12, the RSV's expression, "the rendering of this service," is only a weak reflection of Paul's way of describing the collection. The expression is more literally, "the ministry of this service" (*diakonia tes leitourgias*). The two words are practically synonymous, and they remind us how Paul regarded the collection. *Diakonia* was used for all ministries for others, including the ministry with money. *Leitourgia* was used especially for acts of public service. In Romans 15:27, it is used for those who were "of service" in the collection. The same word is used in Philippians 2:30, where Paul says that Epaphroditus risked his life "to complete your service to me."

A PROMISE TO THE GIVER (9:12-14)

What will be the result of this ministry of giving? We do not want this ministry to be exhausted without any sign of success. When we think of the many challenges to give and the legitimate ministries in which we might wish to take part, we are sure to be reminded that our resources are so meager that they can hardly make a difference. The small resources of our congregation can hardly evangelize the nation. The Corinthians must have asked similar questions about the impact of their small contribution on the service of Jerusalem. Paul responds to these doubts with a reminder of what God can do with our resources. Just as the farmer trusts that his yield will be far greater than what he has planted, our ministry is only a "sowing of seed" (9:6). It is God, and not our resources, who assures a good harvest (9:10).

When Jesus' disciples were faced with five thousand hungry people, they were stunned by Jesus' challenge: "You give them something to eat" (Mark 6:37). Their resources were obviously inadequate for this important undertaking. But Jesus took their insignificant resources and fed the crowd. The result was that "they all ate and were satisfied" (Mark 6:42). Limited resources in his hands were multiplied to God's glory. Paul says that this also happens with our ministries. We not only serve others; our sacrifice is infectious as it "overflows in many thanksgivings to God" (9:12). God's grace is active when we share what we have (9:14).

CONCLUSION

While it may seem "superfluous" (9:1) to continue writing and speaking about money, Paul knew that there is a place for it among authentic disciples. When we speak only of programs and budgets, we lose sight of ministries and forget that we "give ourselves" by giving what we have to others. In the moment that we sacrifice for others, we demonstrate that we have found the "singleness of heart" and the priority of our lives.

10

WHAT HAS RELIGION DONE
FOR YOU?
(6:4-10; 11:16-33)

"Are they servants of Christ? I am a better
one. . . . (11:23).

The American religious experience has been described as "cafeteria-style" religion. Unlike many other countries where one dominant form of religious expression exists, we face an unlimited number of basic approaches of faith. The result of having so many "offerings" is that we become consumers who look for the best bargain. Like good consumers, we shop around until we find the form of ministry that we like. We listen to the claims offered through the media and in different types of literature, and then we make our choice. If we become dissatisfied, we can always change brands!

The question we have been taught to ask of all products is simple: "What shall I get out of it?" "Will its return be commensurate with the costs?" The same kinds of questions are being asked today by individuals and churches. These questions place many churches and ministers in the position of boasting about their offerings. One church offers something for those who look for aesthetic appreciation. Another offers a comfortable place where "peace of mind" can be gotten at a bargain price. Another offers constant signs of spiritual power. Church leaders may even do market research in order to offer a religion that is more attractive than its competitors.

Is it wrong to approach our faith in this way, looking for

what we will "get out of it"? The New Testament does often
speak of what we receive from faith. It does indeed offer peace
of mind, hope, a place of warmth, and spiritual power. But
there are dangers in our "shopping around" to see what each
has to offer. Paul's experience with the Corinthians reminds us
of the dangers of the "consumer" approach to ministry.

A GAME FOR FOOLS
(11:16-22)

The Corinthian Christians were the consumers who were
forced to choose between two types of religion. The "super
apostles" (11:5) and Paul offered very different versions of
Christian ministry. Judging from the criticism of Paul by the
"super apostles," we may assume that their ministry offered
something spectacular (cf. 10:10). They were impressive orators who offered visible demonstrations of the power of God in
their lives. Their ministry was apparently filled with boasting
over their great achievements. Indeed, a striking feature of
chapters 10 through 13 is the frequency of forms of the word
"boast." This word, either in its noun or verb forms, occurs
nineteen times in these chapters. The "super apostles" boasted
of their credentials as men of great spiritual power (cf. 11:22,
18). This boasting placed Paul on the defensive.

The "super apostles" probably boasted of their own "visions
and revelations of the Lord" (12:1), which they offered as signs
of their spiritual power. They criticize Paul for being a weak
figure who travels from city to city, the object of persecution
and scorn. Wherever he goes, he suffers a new defeat, for he is
constantly arrested, beaten, and sent out of town. According
to this view, Paul is incompetent (cf. 2:16) for an important
task. He has left behind a record of weakness and failure.

How do we respond to such charges? We might think that we
can respond best by ignoring criticisms of our ministry. But
Paul does not ignore his critics. We can be happy that Paul
decided not to ignore them, for his answer to these charges
gives the clearest insight in the entire New Testament into the
"mark" of a Christian. Paul decides to match the boast of his

critics in order to defend himself. In 6:4, he provides a list of those marks by which he "commends himself" to his doubters. In 11:16-18, he says that he will now boast himself. He proceeds in 11:22-33 to offer once more the identifying marks of his ministry.

It is, undoubtedly, unpleasant to boast of our identifying marks as servants of Christ. Paul scarcely ever engages in a personal defense of this kind outside of 2 Corinthians. Indeed, he is obviously reticent to discuss such matters. He calls this conversation "foolishness" and concedes that he is playing a game for fools. "I wish you would bear with me in a little foolishness," he says (11:1). He also says, "(What I am saying I say not with as the Lord's authority but as a fool, in this boastful confidence)" (11:17). Under normal circumstances, therefore, the boasting about one's achievements is totally inappropriate. In Paul's words, such boasting is for fools!

Why did Paul, despite his disdain for boasting, decide to engage in boasting himself? "I have been a fool! You forced me to it, . . ." he says (12:11). The Corinthian Christians had gladly listened to fools in the past! He boasted, not to win an argument, but because the Corinthians were confused and easily swayed. With biting sarcasm, he says, "For you bear it if a man makes slaves of you, or preys upon you, or takes advantage of you, or puts on airs, or strikes you in the face" (11:20). If they had been more mature and more capable of distinguishing the true servant of Christ, his boasting would not have been necessary. If they themselves had not been so confused in their approach to ministry, Paul would not have been forced to boast. This church had demonstrated that it would "bear fools gladly."

Paul's conversation with the Corinthians raises some important questions for the life of the contemporary church. If we are consumers in a "cafeteria-style" religion, we are sure to be in a situation similar to that of the Corinthians. We will be offered various and conflicting kinds of ministry from which we can choose, and we will hear the conflicting "boasts" of each. The question we must face is, What are we willing to "put up with"? Paul had played the role of fool because the Corinthians were especially attracted to fools! An important challenge for the church is to know and recognize legitimate ministries and to refuse to be mere consumers. It is possible that we, like the Corinthians, will be impressed by the wrong kinds of claims. We may be attracted to those ministries which offer more results and demand less sacrifice or to the unusual and spectacular ministries. A mature church will not be vulnerable to those who boast only of their extraordinary results.

Other questions arise out of Paul's conversation with the Corinthians. When is it appropriate to boast? And what is worthy of our boast? One kind of boasting is inappropriate, for it leaves the impression that the achievements are our own. The keeping of statistics and records is appropriate, for example. But the fascination with statistics can be for the wrong reason. If we "keep score" only to prove the superiority of our own church, our boasting is inappropriate.

What is worthy of our boast? Paul provides an answer in 11:23-33 and 6:4-10. Every congregation can benefit from Paul's list of the things about which he was willing to boast. It would be worthwhile to compare the things about which he boasts with our own claims.

"ARE THEY HEBREWS? SO AM I"
(11:22)

Paul begins his response by matching the boasts of his critics. "Are they Hebrews? So am I. Are they Israelites? So am I. Are they descendants of Abraham? So am I." We are not certain what distinctions are being made in the terms "Hebrews," "Israelites," and "descendants of Abraham." We only know that the two sides can boast of a pure Jewish heritage. As Paul says in Philippians, he had reason for confidence in the flesh (Philippians 3:3). He could match anyone, boast for boast, on questions of heritage.

At first, it appears that Paul has chosen to boast of the very things of which his critics have boasted. His heritage as a Jew is equal to theirs. But Paul drops the subject! In 11:23-33, he changes the subject to show the proofs that he is a "servant of

Christ" (11:23). Apparently, Paul could match their boasts on the grounds of heritage, but he chooses not to (as in 12:1-10). All of these advantages are now counted as loss "because of the surpassing worth of knowing Christ Jesus" the Lord (Philippians 3:8).

Occasionally, we may boast of that which is relatively trivial. We may point to the leading role which our family has always assumed, to the noble history of our congregation, or to achievements we have made. These are scarcely worthy of boasting. Paul recognizes that he is capable of matching such trivial boasts, but it is hardly worth it.

THE MARKS OF A CHRISTIAN
(11:23-33; 6:4-10)

In two separate passages of 2 Corinthians, Paul lists the facts about his own life which show he is a genuine servant of Christ. "But as servants of God we commend ourselves in every way: ..." (6:4). "Are they servants of Christ? I am a better one. ..." (11:23). Paul, the man accused of being unimpressive and weak, now defends himself. But, to the shock of his audience, he boasts of the very things for which he is criticized. He who was "too weak" to take advantage of the church (11:21) now boasts that which shows his weakness (1:29, 30). Indeed, a key word of chapters 10 through 13 is "weakness," for weakness is a mark of the Christian (cf. 10:10; 12:5, 9, 10; 13:4, 9). The Christian is one who has no power of his own.

Paul has an amazing list of events in his life to demonstrate his weakness. We know of only a few of these instances from Acts or Paul's other letters because he only recalled these events when the validity of his ministry was questioned. These lists give the impression of a pitiful figure who went from one moment of trouble to another.

It is impressive to see where Paul suggests that he has excelled in the Christian life. In 11:23, he repeats expressions like "far greater" and "far more" (*perissoteros* is used both times), along with words like "countless" (*hyperballontos*; NEB, "more severely") and "many times." That is, in one area of his life, he had no equal! It was in the amount of hard work (cf. 6:5; 1 Thessalonians 2:9), imprisonments (cf. 6:5; Acts 16:23), beatings (cf. 6:5) and times when he was near death (cf. 1:8-11). In these moments, he looked like a pitiful and helpless figure. No miraculous signs of God's favor appeared for a helpless man who had been beaten and left to die. No one was likely to see in such distasteful incidents the signs of God's power.

We are amazed as we read of the helplessness of Paul, the extraordinary variety of injuries he had borne, and the number of painful moments in his life. The effect of reading the list is to notice that Paul's ministry, instead of offering health, wealth, and peace of mind, brought him nothing but pain. Extreme moments of physical pain are described in 11:24, 25. The traditional Jewish "thirty-nine lashes," which Paul received five times, was both painful and humiliating. The beating with rods (cf. Acts 16:37; 22:25, 29) was a Roman punishment; the stoning (cf. Acts 14:19) was done by a lynch mob. Everywhere Paul went, he created a public disturbance that led to a humiliating beating by officials and by angry mobs. As Galatians 6:17 suggests, Paul wore "the marks of Jesus" on him in literal battle scars.

Besides actual beatings and lynch mobs, there were the constant dangers of more trouble. In 11:26, the word "danger" is repeated several times to show the variety of physical perils. The dangers were associated with travel in an era when the traveler faced disaster both from nature ("danger from rivers," "danger at sea") and from roaming bandits. The danger could be as exhausting as the actual presence of trouble.

Hardships also came from having no guaranteed salary, disability, or unemployment benefits. Having made his profession a secondary matter and having depended always on gifts that came irregularly from others, Paul faced hunger and thirst, cold and exposure (11:27). He had voluntarily accepted extraordinary insecurities because he trusted that God would provide. Ministry had involved a decision to sacrifice a standard of living in order to place his life at God's disposal. He had learned "in any and all circumstances" the secret of "facing plenty and hunger, abundance and want" (Philippians 4:12). He had said earlier in 2 Corinthians, "As sorrowful, yet always rejoicing; as poor, yet making many rich; as having nothing, and yet possessing everything" (6:10)! Ministry had involved risks of personal financial security and a wealth that could not be measured.

Paul's physical condition was no advertisement for a consumer-oriented public. His kind of Christianity had gotten him into much trouble. No one who was shopping around for the one which offered the most benefits would have been attracted by this form of Christianity.

ANXIETY FOR ALL THE CHURCHES
(11:28)

Paul's ministry had involved more than beatings and lynch mobs. Another pain might have been more severe: "Apart from other things, there is the daily pressure upon me of my anxiety for all the churches" (11:28). In authentic ministry, problems can never be left at the office! Paul did not claim that his ministry even brought him peace of mind. There was "daily pressure" (*epistasis*). The word might be rendered "the burden of oversight." Ministry involved sleepless nights (11:27; cf. "watching" in 6:5). No one who is involved in Christian service can preach the gospel and assist in the founding of a church and then simply walk away!

Paul's "anxiety for all the churches" reflects the fact that his missionary labors resulted in the formation of churches throughout the Mediterranean world. His letters and his return visits remind us that he remained deeply involved in their lives. He agonized over a divided church. He expressed shock and bitter disappointment when some of them deserted the gospel (Galatians 1:6). He maintained the best communications possible. He was always willing to struggle with the recurring problems of the churches. Paul felt personally responsible, not only for being present at the birth of a new church. He was like an anxious father of the bride who wishes to be sure that his daughter is protected and preserved (11:2).

He was like the concerned parent who watches over his children (12:14). No one in this situation can walk away from his "anxiety for all the churches."

Those who approach the Christian faith as mere consumers will not be comfortable with a Christianity which involves "anxiety for all the churches." We want a religion that takes away our anxiety, and not one which produces it! We want a Christian life that is tranquil and serene, not one that gives us sleepless nights. We often choose our home congregation because of its potential of offering escape from problems. But Paul knew that we cannot escape the problems which cause us deep concern. Paul's statement in 11:28 suggests that one of the marks of a genuine Christian is this concern over the church's problems.

It is only natural for most of us to wish to "choose a winner" when we involve ourselves in the life of a church. Some move from church to church, hoping to escape the problems of one church and to choose one that has no problems. In the congregations I have known, others remained and struggled with a church torn by internal friction. Others remained committed to churches that seemed to be suffering the woes of a declining neighborhood. Some Christians always chose "anxiety for all the churches" rather than walk away from the problems of troubled communities.

A HUMILIATING MOMENT
(11:32, 33)

One humiliating moment in Paul's career stood out. It was the time in Damascus when Paul escaped the city guards by being let down in a basket through a window in the wall. The moment was not recalled because of the physical torture involved. It was remembered because Paul had been a ridiculous-looking figure being let down in a basket. The scene of a grown man escaping in a basket might have even looked humorous to an onlooker. The Christians who were left behind could scarcely point with pride to the "grand style" in which their leader left town! Opponents of Paul could point to this moment as an example of Paul as a weak figure who was an embarrassment to the church.

In the ancient world, the finest military award for valor was the medal given to the man who was the first up the wall in the face of the enemy. Paul portrays himself as the exact opposite: He was the first down the wall. He had no demonstration of power and no electrifying speech to sway the crowd. Paul dared to boast of the crowning humiliation of his life, an event that was probably being told by his enemies who were wanting to discredit him. Surely, they thought, no one who is humiliated and beaten can display the power of God in his ministry.

Paul had begun this entire defense of his ministry (11:16-33) by "playing the fool" and matching his critics boast for boast (11:16-22). We may assume that they had their own list of victories. But in 11:23-33, Paul finds it unnatural to match their boasting of their achievements. He offers, instead, a list of hard times and failures. The weakness for which he is ridiculed is the very thing of which he boasts. "Who is weak, and I am not weak?" he asks. "If I must boast, I will boast of the things that show my weakness" (11:30). Paul refused to use the world's standard of success for defending his ministry. His ministry was characterized by hard work, sleepless nights, and challenges that were beyond his strength.

His answer was not popular then, and it is unlikely to be popular now. We have other lists which we offer to validate our ministries. We seldom list our weaknesses in our resumes and year-end reports. Imagine the congregation which would look favorably on Paul's list of achievements on a minister's record. A church that is modeled on the corporation will demand the signs of success. Paul's list reminds us that some successful ministries have never been brought to our attention. It is possible that some "successful" ministries are not successful by Paul's standards.

STRENGTH IN WEAKNESS

When we comprehend the mental and physical beatings that Paul took in his life, we are amazed that this fragile "earthen vessel" survived at all. The inadequate medical care, the beatings, the exposure, the irregular diet, and the constant travel under dangerous circumstances were enough to exhaust the most robust athlete. The "many times" that he came near death must have left lingering scars, if not disabilities. The list of Paul's "weaknesses" amazes us, therefore, with Paul's extraordinary strength to endure. Countless moments of physical and emotional exhaustion came when Paul's strength was exhausted. But he always found a reserve of power that came from God. In pouring out his strength, he was being resupplied by God.

CONCLUSION

Perhaps a major reason why we have lacked a sustaining power in our own ministries is that a "cafeteria-style" religion always looks to those who claim to revolutionize our congregations at bargain prices. We, like the Corinthians, like to keep score on our achievements without great risks to a comfortable lifestyle. Paul does not offer the lifestyle that is comfortable. The power of authentic ministry comes, not from the most creative programs, but from exhausting ourselves for the sake of the cause of Christ. "When we are weak, then we are strong." The mark of the Christian is the weakness that is open to God's power.

11

OUT OF THIS WORLD
(12:1-12)

"... I will not boast, except in my weaknesses" (12:5).

The mark of a genuine Christian life, according to a popular view, is the quality of experience that we might describe as "out of this world." This kind of experience is often measured, analyzed, and offered as a sign of authentic discipleship. Sometimes, those who place their emphasis on what is "out of this world" compare their experiences with each other in order to demonstrate the genuineness of their Christian life. The guest on the religious talk show may offer as evidence of God's presence the prayer which resulted in finding a new job. In some circles, the test of the Christian life is the intensity of the emotional excitement, the feelings of power, and the enthusiasm by which people are "carried away." The one test that is applied to every period of worship becomes, Was it "out of this world"?

This particular test of the genuineness of our faith reminds us of the continuing relevance of the New Testament for our questions, for the same kind of questions were being raised by the Corinthians. When Paul wrote 2 Corinthians, his genuineness as a Christian (10:7) and as a servant of Christ (11:23) was being questioned. Some, having noticed how unimpressive he was, demanded "proof" that Christ was actually speaking in him (13:3). Such an unimpressive speaker, they assumed, could not possibly be a spiritual man. If he had been endowed with the Spirit, they thought, some "sign of a true apostle" (cf. 12:11, 12) would be evident to demonstrate his genuineness.

Paul's genuineness as a servant of Christ was apparently questioned by those who were called "superlative apostles" (12:11). Someone had probably denied that the "signs of a true apostle" were in Paul, for his opponents were intent on "comparing themselves" and "measuring themselves" with Paul (cf. 10:12). Paul's insistence that he had performed "the signs of a true apostle" suggests that he is on the defensive. Others have boasted of their own miracles and "signs" and have compared their experiences with Paul's. Many of their experiences were "out of this world." Paul's term in 5:13, "besides ourselves" (*exestemen*), is literally "ecstatic." For some, the test of authenticity was in ecstatic and emotional experience. These "signs" proved that one had the Spirit of God.

CAUGHT UP TO THE THIRD HEAVEN (12:1-6)

Those who tested the genuineness of others' spirituality on the basis of ecstasy and emotional experience have their representatives in our own time. They force us to ask, "What role does the "out of this world" experience have in the Christian life? Are we to assume that it is the test of our genuineness? Or are we to suspect all emotional experience and conclude that it has no place in the Christian life? Paul's reply helps us to answer these questions.

The content of 12:1-6 is unlike anything else that Paul ever wrote. He reports about experiences which he never mentions anywhere else. The reason for this unusual material is obvious: Paul only discusses these experiences because others have forced him to discuss them. He knows that such reports sound like boasting and that "there is nothing to be gained by it" (12:1). "You forced me to it," he says (12:11). Such boasting is foolish (11:16, 17, 21), but necessary (12:1) in this situation. If others had not forced the subject, Paul would never have reported on these intimate details of his life. He takes up the subject of "visions and revelations of the Lord" only because he must match his critics boast for boast.

Because 12:1-10 is unique in Paul's letters, many of us are amazed to discover that Paul did not rule out experiences that are "out of this world." There were "visions and revelations of the Lord" (12:1). This reference reminds us naturally of the time of his conversion, which is described both as a vision (Acts 26:19) and a revelation (Galatians 1:12). But Paul's extraordinary experiences did not end at his conversion. There was an "abundance of the revelations" (12:7), some of which have been recorded in Acts (9:12; 16:19; 18:9-11). This subject reminds us of 1 Corinthians 14:18, where Paul says, "I thank God that I speak in tongues more than you all." Paul knew what it meant to be "beside himself" (5:13) for Christ. His critics had no deep spiritual experience which was unknown to Paul.

It is not inaccurate to say that such moments were important to Paul. In fact, he recalls one particular instance of a vision that has been unforgettable. This extraordinary moment occurred fourteen years before the writing of 2 Corinthians (ca. A.D. 42). Paul speaks of an experience that was literally "out of this world." He was "caught up to the third heaven" and "caught up into Paradise" (12:2, 3). The experience reminds us of the stories of Enoch (Genesis 5:24) and Elijah (2 Kings 2:11). The Greek word for "caught up" (*harpzao*) indicates that the whole experience was not initiated by Paul. Such extraordinary experiences were apparently common to him. In 2 Corinthians, he refers to their "abundance." It had not been brought on by special techniques or preparation or by Paul's own powers of suggestion. The word means literally "seized" or "carried off." Paul did not doubt that God had acted to grant him this experience "out of this world."

What Paul remembered most was that he "heard things that cannot be told, which man may not utter" (12:4). What Paul heard was beyond the capacity of human speech to express. Paul's word remind us of his earlier references to the "tongues of angels" (1 Corinthians 13:1) and the spiritual gifts of 1 Corinthians 12—14. In 1 Corinthians 2:9 he speaks of those things which "no eye has seen, nor ear heard." These things are revealed through God's Spirit, which allows us to know the mind of God (1 Corinthians 2:11, 12). Some words were beyond human speech. Paul had experienced many visions and revelations, but one was particularly unforgettable. Paul's Christian ministry involved moments of inexpressible spiritual ecstacy. He could claim as much as his critics could claim.

We would naturally expect someone who had experienced such an amazing story to describe it in its most exact details. We would not be surprised to see a great visionary devote an entire book to an analysis of the total experience. What did it feel like? How long did it last? But this fascination with the details is missing in Paul's description. He does not look back and recall his bodily sensations. ("Whether in the body or out of the body I do not know.") All that he knows is that he was "caught up" by God. Paul did not keep a journal in order to boast about his spiritual achievements. Just as he did not keep records of his baptisms (1 Corinthians 1:16), he did not keep records of his visions and revelations.

Probably because Paul is uncomfortable in boasting about his spiritual achievements, he chooses to speak of "a man in Christ" (12:2) and of "this man" (12:3). "This man" is Paul himself, as 12:7 makes clear. But Paul knows that these great moments are not his own. It was not because of anything that he had done that he could recall "out of this world" experiences. As he said in 10:17, "Let him who boasts, boast of the Lord." It was not Paul's psychic powers or his unique capacity for spiritual experience that led to his "visions and revelations of the Lord"; it was his relationship to Christ. Thus, all of these experiences were nothing to boast about! Paul describes these moments in his life because others have brought up the subject. He relates experiences "that cannot be told" in order to say that he does not offer them as proof of his discipleship!

Paul never rejected the deep spiritual and emotional experiences. He always says suggested that it was inappropriate to parade his experiences before others. To analyze and compare such experiences would be inappropriate. He said, "For if we are beside ourselves, it is for God; . . ." (5:13). Such moments were between himself and God, not for the whole community.

In a similar context, Paul said that when Christians spoke in tongues, they spoke to God (1 Corinthians 14:2). Although he himself spoke in tongues, it was a matter between himself and God (1 Corinthians 14:18). In the presence of the whole church, he preferred to speak five intelligible words than to parade his own spiritual experiences (1 Corinthians 14:19).

Paul was willing to say that extraordinary moments of being "caught up" had a place in his life, but he was unwilling to offer those experiences as "proof" of his apostleship. His critics had undoubtedly boasted of having the "signs of a true apostle" (12:12). While Paul was willing to match their "signs," he would not offer them as proof of his claims. He says, "On behalf of this man I will boast, but on my own behalf I will not boast, except of my weaknesses" (12:5). In fact, the evidence of "out of this world" experiences leads to deception (cf. 12:6). People who offer these claims may either deceive themselves or others (11:13-15). Many people can claim the experience that is "out of this world." It would be impossible to accept every claim as proof of one's discipleship.

We can assume that one who had "an abundance of revelations" must have had many other stories to tell. Indeed, some delight in entertaining us with such stories. But Paul refrains from such boasting (12:6) because he chooses to be tested by the evidence that is before the Corinthians' eye (cf. 10:7; 11:6). The proof of Paul's apostleship is not the peak emotional experience, but the record which he has left behind. His weakness, which had been the subject of much criticism, had not prevented him from changing lives. Where the gospel is believed and the church is founded, God is at work. The ultimate test of our discipleship is what others "can see and hear"—the acts of service which demonstrate our concern for others, our record of denying ourselves for others, the times when our commitment to the life of the church is seen by others. Those who emphasize the peak experiences may become so fascinated with their own emotions that they ignore the needs of others.

The rival claims of Paul and his opponents about peak experiences probably sound far removed for most of us, for scarcely anyone today claims to share in such amazing experiences. Nevertheless, we do face similar questions. We speak of "mountaintop experiences" and of being "carried away." We ask what place the emotions have in our Christian lives. Some look with dismay on all worship that appeals to the emotions. Others submit all religious experience to the test of the emotions and demand that it must be "out of this world." Paul's answer to the question is appropriate for us. There is a place for the peak experience, but it is never the ultimate test of our Christianity. The emotions may deceive us. But Paul's test of loving service over an extended period will not deceive us.

ANOTHER EXPERIENCE: POWER AND WEAKNESS (12:7-10)

One of the "proofs" commonly offered for the presence of God's power and for the genuineness of our discipleship is the evidence that is offered for prayers that have been answered. Some suggest that we can always point to the concrete things that our religion has done for us. In answer to prayer, we are often told, God opens doors to financial success and ensures us of health and peace of mind. Indeed, in some instances, people have compared results in order to prove the truth of their faith.

No Christian would deny that God listens to and answers prayer. But it is possible that we can misunderstand prayer and treat it as some kind of magic formula for satisfying our desires. Paul's critics, in their fascination with boasting about their peak experiences, had probably boasted also of the marvelous effects of prayer. We do not know what they claim, but Paul's description of his own prayer life suggests that he is again prepared to match their boasts. Perhaps they had described prayer as a time when they experienced God's power in a special way.

Paul begins his story about prayer by recalling another instance in his life that is otherwise unknown to us. His Christian life, he tells us, was not composed only of peak experiences. In order to keep him from being too elated, God sent him a "thorn in the flesh" to "harass" him (12:7). God had taken him from the heights of ecstasy in Paradise to the realities of pain on earth. The same one who had been "caught up" had been humbled by pain. The pain counterbalanced the ecstatic moment. Although the suggested solutions have been numerous, we do not know what Paul's "thorn in the flesh" was. The possibilities include either a speech impediment (cf. 10:10) or an eye disease (cf. Galatians 4:15). In the early church, some thought that Paul's ailment was epilepsy. Such guesses are probably useless. All we know is that the "thorn in the flesh" gave Paul both physical and emotional pain. The word rendered "harass" in the RSV was the word meaning "to strike with the fist." It was commonly used for beatings (cf. 1 Peter 2:20). It could refer to the effects of persecution on Paul's physical health. In this context, the "thorn in the flesh" was an example of Paul's physical weakness, that limitation which many thought was enough to discredit him. It would have been easy to allow the great experiences to "go to his head" and to cause him to become puffed up—the error of the "superlative apostles"(10:12f.). Instead, a physical ailment reminded him of his weakness and dependence on God's grace.

We might expect someone of Paul's spiritual power to tell us of his great victory over pain that came through prayer. In fact, in this context we are expecting Paul to relate another example of great spiritual victory. Others have probably offered their own versions of moments when they were enabled through prayer to overcome great obstacles. But what amazes us in 12:7, 8 is that Paul tells no such story. If his readers were expecting him to tell of easy solutions and impressive power through prayer, they were disappointed. "Three times I besought the Lord about this, that it should leave me" (12:8). The answer did not come on his first or even his second prayer. "Three times" suggests the special intensity of a prayer (cf. Mark 14:32-39) when there are no quick and magic answers.

Paul's request concerning the "thorn in the flesh" was never answered to fit his plea. The only answer he received was, "My grace is sufficient for you, for my power is made perfect in weakness" (12:9). He was forced to continue his missionary labors in fragile health. He had probably thought many times that his effectiveness could have been increased greatly if only his health were better. He could have impressed more people with his personal appearance and his stamina if only he could demonstrate great power! Nevertheless, Paul could not point to prayers that offered the "proof" of God's power.

There is another reference to Paul's fragile health in Galatians 4:13, where he says, "You know it was because of a bodily ailment that I preached the gospel to you at first." We do not know the circumstances of that first missionary preaching, but we are impressed by the fact that the Galatians might never have heard Paul if it had not been for his sickness. God was able to use him precisely because of his illness! That bodily ailment was never able to stop Paul. It only changed his schedule and directed him to change his plans.

It was during this experience of enduring the "thorn in the flesh" that Paul learned a valuable lesson. The "proof" of our Christianity is not in our peak experiences or in the instances where prayer "worked." These experiences lead us to boast of our own achievements. The authentic Christian knows that he depends, not on himself, but on the grace of God. "My grace is sufficient for you, for my power is made perfect in weakness." God was able to use Paul, not despite his weakness, but because of his weakness.

There was no greater sign of God's power than the existence of churches throughout the Mediterranean world. These churches, founded by an unimpressive figure in a world which admired visible rhetorical and physical power, were the midst of human weakness. If the founder of these churches had possessed the common "proofs" of power, many would have failed to see God's power at work in the world. They would have concluded that human power was at work in the world.

It is fascinating that Paul placed the two very different accounts of his own experience together in this context. One instance described moments of amazing spiritual power. The other described an "embarrassing failure" for a spiritual leader. It is the latter which is the "proof" of Paul's genuineness, for he will not boast of anything but his weaknesses. He said in 12:5 that he did not care to boast of "this man," for he only wished to boast of his weaknesses. In 12:9, he repeats the same thought: ". . . I will all the more gladly boast of my weaknesses, that the power of Christ may rest upon me."

WEAKNESS AND POWER (12:10-12)

We must admit that Paul's approach to weakness and power runs contrary to our natural inclinations. We would prefer to say, "When I am strong, then I am strong," for this is the standard of our culture. We know books on self-assertiveness are always popular because they appeal to our fascination with power. If our natural inclinations affect our Christian life, we will see our ministry in this perspective. When we think of a successful minister or successful church, we may look for the signs of power and influence. We may encourage a system where ministers and church leaders are forced to compare results that point to their resourcefulness. We can be tempted to believe that no genuine ministry is possible unless we have the symbols of power: the magnificent building, the latest equipment, the most creative personnel, and the greatest members. It is certainly appropriate to have good facilities and talented people. But we deceive ourselves if we conclude that our own strength is neccessary before God's power can have its effect.

Under prevailing standards, Jesus and His disciples were absolutely powerless. The cross symbolized human weakness. But His weakness at the cross was the occasion for the power of the resurrection. Paul says, "For he was crucified in weakness, but lives by the power of God" (13:4). Out of his weakness came God's power. In authentic discipleship, we cannot ignore that weakness is strength. Paul learned from his "thorn in the flesh" that God's power is perfected in weaknesses (12:9). For this reason he was content with "weaknesses, insults, hardships, persecutions, and calamities." He concludes, ". . . for when I am weak, then I am strong" (12:10).

What is the mark of a successful ministry? The successful ministry can be seen where the miracle of the cross and resur- rection is repeated. When our weakness provides the opportunity for God's power to work, we become a successful church. It is impressive in 12:10-13 that Paul boasts repeatedly of the very weakness for which he had been criticized (11:30; 12:5, 9; cf. 13:4). His critics had looked to the wrong "signs of a true apostle" (12:12).

CONCLUSION

Perhaps we often stand in the place of Paul's critics, looking to the wrong signs of true Christianity. The peak experiences are more impressive and exciting. They are undoubtedly more attractive to the outsider. They provide, as with Paul, unforgettable memories. But a true church does not stay "out of this world." The final test of its loyalty is its willingness to live where there is pain and frustration. These are very much "in the world."

12

ANOTHER JESUS, ANOTHER MINISTRY
(3:1-3; 11:1-22)

"I feel a divine jealousy for you, . . ." (11:2).

In 1925, the Chicago businessman Bruce Barton wrote a popular book on Jesus, entitled, *The Man Nobody Knows.* Jesus was portrayed as a businessman who had all of the traits necessary to build a great organization. Barton noticed that Jesus, at the age of twelve, had said, "I must be about my father's business" (Luke 2:49; KJV). From that time on, Jesus had all of the characteristics which the Chicago businessman held in esteem. His habit of rising early (Mark 1:35) indicated that He was a "go-getter." His frequent appearances at wedding parties (John 2:1-11) and dinners (cf. Luke 14:1, 7, 12, 15) suggested that He had the active social life necessary for advancement. His parables demonstrated a gift for words and His mastery of the techniques of advertising. According to Barton, Jesus was the perfect model of the young man on the way to the top. He was sociable and pleasant, the kind of man who knew how to become popular.

Partial truths are seen in this portrayal of Jesus. The author did not exactly ignore the Gospel accounts. Nevertheless, we cannot avoid the conclusion that the author chose his Scriptures selectively in order to "make Jesus in his own image." This portrayal fit what the author and thousands of readers wanted to see in Jesus. He represented their values and ideals.

The highest value to the author was the attainment of success and popularity. Consequently, he represented Jesus as the embodiment of these values.

Do we not all try to portray Jesus as one so much like ourselves that we ignore those aspects of His ministry that do not fit our point of view? Artists have always portrayed Him with the features common to their culture. To Europeans, Jesus has been portrayed with European features; to Asians He has looked Asian. The representatives of the different political philosophies have also tried to "make Jesus in their own image." Capitalists have pictured Him as a capitalist, while socialists have portrayed Him as a socialist. Those who have called for rapid change have thought of Jesus as one like themselves; those who have wanted to maintain the status quo have also thought of Him as one who shared their values. It is possible that we, too, often think of Jesus as one who shares the point of view that is common in our culture.

The problem of "making Jesus in our own image" is that those who model Jesus after themselves cannot possibly model themselves after Jesus! We can distort His message so much that it becomes indistinguishable from the latest fad in popular psychology or any of the various "isms." Unless we recognize in Jesus a whole new world of values, we cannot be changed ourselves. Unless we see Him as the one who upsets the values of our culture, the ministry of the church will be no different from the work of any other institution. Without someone who opens up to us a new world of values, we lose our identity as a church.

GODLY JEALOUSY (11:1, 2; 3:1-3)

To Paul, it was particularly important that the church at Corinth maintain its identity, for he was especially involved with that church. "I feel a divine jealousy for you," he says (11:2; NIV, "godly jealousy"). He was not jealous for this church for his own sake. As the minister who had founded this church, it was not personal loyalty that he prized. His jealousy was God's jealousy. The language reminds us of the common portrayal of God in the Old Testament as the jealous One who would tolerate no rivals (Deuteronomy 4:24; 5:9). He had selected His people to be His special possession, and He had poured out His love for them (Deuteronomy 7:6-11). The "jealous God" demanded from His people only what He was willing to give: the steadfast love and devoted faithfulness that would never end. Sometimes the Old Testament describes this "jealous God" in realistic and graphic terms as the devoted bridegroom whose love will never let go. (See Hosea 1—3; Ezekiel 16.) Despite the unfaithfulness of His "spouse," God never contemplates divorce (Isaiah 50:1), for He is steadfastly committed to His bride. This God pursues His bride single-mindedly, always calling for her to return this steadfast love.

Paul shares God's jealousy, for he has much at stake in being certain that the Corinthians return God's faithful love: "For I betrothed you to Christ to present you as a pure bride to her one husband" (11:2). Paul shares God's jealousy because he was present at the wedding! As an attendant at the wedding, Paul was responsible for the survival of the marriage. The image of betrothal suggests that Paul is actually the father of the bride. He looks back on their conversion as the time of their betrothal, the moment when they took their vows of fidelity. Now the one who was responsible for the engagement is personally committed to see that the bride retains her purity until the day of the wedding (cf. Ephesians 5:22, 23; Revelation 19:7).

Paul's image of the betrothal is a striking reminder of the strong sense of commitment to the churches which was a part of his ministry. It is not uncommon for him to try to motivate his churches to faithfulness by recalling their conversion. When the Galatian church was faltering over false teaching, Paul wrote to remind them of the joyous days when they first heard the gospel: "What has become of the satisfaction you felt? For I bear you witness that, if possible, you would have plucked out your eyes and given them to me" (Galatians 4:15). Then he describes himself as one who is in the pains of child-birth (Galatians 4:19) for the sake of the church. To the Corinthians, he writes, ". . . for I became your father in Christ Jesus through the gospel" (1 Corinthians 4:15). According to the imagery, Paul is the bride's father and the father and mother of the church at the same time. The future of the church concerns him deeply, for he had both "betrothed" and "given birth" to them.

Paul uses a different image for his work in founding the church in 3:1-3. Here, he is apparently defending himself for not having the proper credentials for ministry. False apostles have come with impressive letters of recommendation. Paul is challenged to produce his own letter. Paul's answer is simple: "You yourselves are our letter of recommendation" (3:2). This means their very existence is evidence of his work. What other credentials could he need? He says, "And you show that you are a letter from Christ delivered by us" (3:3). The word "delivered" is literally "ministered." The NIV renders the verse appropriately: "You show that you are a letter, a result of our ministry. . . ." He had played a vital role in this existence. Without his ministry, this church would never have come into existence.

What is the mark of true ministry? We can learn much from the images Paul uses for his ministry. Authentic service involves more than programs to be administered. More is involved than efficient organizing capabilities, more even than powerful preaching. The mark of authentic ministry is the recognition that we are not finished with our task when we "betroth" someone to Christ or "give birth" to a new Christian. The authentic Christian is one who is willing to accept the responsibilities of parenthood—the pain and anxious concern of watching over children year after year. Any parent knows that at no point can he simply walk away from his children after bringing them into the world. A parent's concern does not diminish with the years. Authentic ministry involves more than the joy of new births; it involves the anxious concern and care of watching the children grow to maturity.

No one would measure the success of parents on the basis of their first year (or first few years of parenthood. The results of our parenthood are recognized decades later. Paul indicates that the authenticity of his ministry will be recognized only in the results of his work at places like Corinth. Others may rely on their credentials that are written with pen and ink, but Paul knows that the real test of his ministry is what he leaves behind: "You yourselves are our letter of recommendation" (3:2). The community itself is the final proof of his work. Throughout the Mediterranean world, changed lives and strong churches were Paul's only credentials. Paul knew that the real test of his work was the fate of a church after first betrothal. Thus, he could not easily let go.

Perhaps we have commonly overlooked one of the real marks of ministry. We have frequently been interested in recording the "betrothals," for they are easier to record than the final results. We have measured mission programs by the number of "betrothals" registered. When we speak of results, we often consider only the preliminary results—the beginnings of churches and the new births in Christ. Paul knew that his task as father of the bride was unfinished until the final result, the time at the end when the bride would be presented to Christ. He could not be satisfied with the preliminary results.

How do we judge the effectiveness of a program in the church which produces no immediate results? Our "letter of recommendation" is what we finally leave behind. The real results are not necesarily known immediately. True ministry involves sharing God's jealousy in determining that the betrothal will never be broken by infidelity, but will finally be concluded with a wedding.

ANXIOUS MOMENTS (11:3, 4)

The father of the bride, according to Paul, is sure to have anxious moments. On more than one occasion, Paul refers to his anxiety (11:28) or his fear (cf. 12:20) on the church's behalf. In 11:3, he refers once more to this fear. It is possible that the "betrothal," for which he had labored, would come to nothing. There is the memory that, since the beginning of time, good beginnings were no insurance against failure. The church, like Eve in the beginning, is tempted by a foe who is capable of "seducing" his victim by his "cunning" (cf. 4:2; 12:16 for the same Greek word, *panourgia*). The word rendered "cunning" in the RSV (*panourgia*) means literally, "do anything" or "stop at nothing." The seducer has no limits to his resources in beguiling the innocent bride. The arguments of this adversary are often persuasive and attractive. He is the third party who delights in "leading astray" or "seducing" his prey from her single-minded devotion to the future husband. This possibility gives every servant of Christ anxious moments.

Paul's anxious moments did not come from unfounded worry. According to 11:4, some were already preaching to the readers "another Jesus," "another Spirit," and "another gospel." The final results of Paul's work were very much in doubt. The church had a record of "submitting to" (literally, "putting up with") those who attempted to entice them. The father of the bride had good reasons for fearing that the wedding would never take place. The church was being seduced. It was as if she were turning away from her future spouse for a new lover.

In one sense, there is no other gospel (Galatians 1:7). But there are distortions of the one gospel, phony faiths which "seduce" Christians away from their loyalty to Christ. The most "cunning" and beguiling manner of seduction is not the one which attacks the faith; those who were seducing the Corinthians had not come to attack the faith. Indeed they spoke in the name of Jesus, and they "preached the gospel." But "another Jesus" and "different gospel" is what they preached. We suspect that the "other Jesus" whom they preached was a reflection of themselves! Perhaps they regarded Jesus from "a worldly point of view," as Paul once had before he became a Christian (5:16, 17). Paul had preached "Christ crucified" to the Corinthians (1 Corinthians 1:23). He had told them about the one who was "crucified in weakness" (13:4). Paul's portrayal of Jesus was not one that was in tune with the spirit of the age. No one wanted to hear about the one who suffered on a cross. They preferred "another Jesus," one who fit the tastes of the audience.

Someone has said that "whoever marries the spirit of the age is sure to be left an early widow." The seduction of the church in every age is the desire to follow "another Jesus," one who is in tune with the spirit of that age. Discipleship seems easier if only we can "make Jesus in our own image." The church which preaches "another Jesus" may be immensely popular, for its ministries will be tailored to fit the tastes of the audience. Like good advertisers, churches may base their proclamation on the "market research" which determines what the audience wants to hear.

Authentic ministry involves recognizing that the church can always be seduced from her single-minded devotion to her husband. Paul indicates elsewhere in his letters that the possibility of falling away exists. More than a year before, he wrote 1 Corinthians, saying, "Therefore let any one who thinks that he stands take heed lest he fall" (1 Corinthians 10:12). He was filled with disappointment because the Galatians had "deserted" the one who had called them (Galatians 1:6). To maintain a "sincere and pure devotion to Christ" (11:3) is no easy task, for the other "suitors" are always attractive and cunning.

This "seduction" does not always take the form of a strange doctrine. Christians may, in fact, be vulnerable to this deception while being well fortified against false doctrines. We could be doctrinally correct on important points and, nevertheless, be seduced by the gods of power, selfishness, and materialism. Furthermore, we may say the right words and participate in the right functions and be enticed by the glamor of success. The pure bride does more than say the right words; she is not enticed by anything which hinders single-minded devotion to the one who has called her. It is not only false doctrine that destroys our commitments. We can also be enticed by other commitments which take away our "pure devotion to Christ."

ANOTHER JESUS AND ANOTHER KIND OF MINISTRY (11:6)

Does it matter how we portray Jesus? Paul's condemnation of those who proclaim "another Jesus" shows that it does matter whether or not we know Jesus. It matters because our view of Jesus determines the nature of our ministry. If we view Jesus from a worldly point of view (cf. 5:16), our ministries will also be judged by worldly standards. If we think of Jesus as the ultimate crowd pleaser and showman, our ministries will reflect that view. If Jesus is remembered for his enormous organizational abilities, our ministry will be modeled after that view of Jesus.

It is not accidental that, in the same context where Paul expresses his anxiety that the church might be enticed by those who offered "another Jesus," he once more insists that he is not inferior to the "superlative apostles" (11:5). According to 11:6, a sign of Paul's inferiority had been his inability as a speaker. He had impressed no one with evidence that he was richly endowed as a powerful speaker (cf. 10:10). Those who had preached "another Jesus" looked for signs of power in his servants. It was only logical to them that a real servant of Christ would be an overwhelming speaker. This criticism of Paul indicates that the "other Jesus" embodied for Paul's critics all of the qualities that were highly esteemed then. Jesus represented power and glory. They had modeled themselves after "another Jesus." The "other Jesus" was immensely popular; he represented "bargain basement" religion. Those who preached "another Jesus" told the audiences what they wanted to hear.

The mark of Paul's ministry was neither his showmanship nor his impressive presence. The mark of Paul's life, according to 11:8, was *diakonia*, "service." He had "abased himself" by taking no money from the Corinthians. The NIV renders Paul's words appropriately, "I lowered myself." Paul notably is referring to the fact that he had worked with his hands during his ministry in Corinth. In a world where a dignified man—and particularly a teacher—would not have "lowered himself" by getting his hands dirty, Paul pointed to his willingness to work with his hands as the mark of his ministry (cf. 1 Corinthians 4:12). To others, this refusal to burden others was undoubtedly a sign of weakness; to Paul it was a sign of true ministry. True ministry involves "lowering ourselves" in order to serve others (11:7-11).

HUMILIATED OR EXALTED (11:7-15)

The mark of Paul's ministry was neither his showmanship nor his impressive appearance. The mark of Paul's life, according to 11:8, was *diakonia*, "service" for his church. Paul was not the only one who called himself " minister" and "apostle," for his opponents had taken those distinguished titles and applied them to themselves (11:12-15). According to Paul, however, the titles were nothing more than a disguise (11:14). The opponents of Paul are reminders that authentic ministry consists of more than using the right titles and saying the right words. Satan's most significant achievements may be made under the disguise of the correct words.

The opponents of Paul had distinguished themselves as demanding and overbearing. Paul says, "For you bear it if a man makes slaves of you, or preys upon you, or takes advantage of you, or puts on airs, or strikes you in the face" (11:20). The subject which Paul addresses in 11:7-11 suggests that the opponents were demanding their rights to receive financial support. Apparently, someone has criticized Paul for not receiving financial support. "Could his custom of not insisting on his rights to financial support be a sign that he has his own doubts about the value of his work?" they asked. "See how he abases himself!" they seemed to say.

The action, not the title, distinguishes authentic ministry. Paul had indeed "abased himself" by not insisting on his right to financial support. To Paul, it was a sign of authentic ministry. True ministry involves "lowering ourselves" to serve others.

CONCLUSION

The Jesus whom Paul preached was "crucified in weakness" (13:4). His culture had regarded him as a weak and insignificant figure. But Paul had learned not to look at Jesus from a "human point of view." Paul did not model his ministry after the "other Jesus," and he did not in his own ministry reflect the values of his culture. Paul's ministry was modeled after the "man for others." Rather than make Jesus in his own image,

Paul's ministry demonstrated that he had been conformed to the image of the crucified Lord.

13

ON PASSING THE TEST
(12:14—13:10)

"And I will most gladly spend and be spent for your souls. . . ." (12:15).

In our culture, one of the major symbols of achievement is diplomas. We make great sacrifices for ourselves and for our children for the sake of the diploma or for other certificates of achievement. We place great emphasis on diplomas and certificates because they are connected with certain "rights and privileges" which our society confers. Before we can teach school, practice medicine or law, or work in many areas of industry, we must present the credentials to demonstrate that we have been examined and certified.

I doubt if most of us would want to change this emphasis on diplomas and certificates. We would not want to entrust our lives to a "self-appointed" physician. Nor would we want to place the education of our children in the hands of someone who had never been examined. We accept this emphasis on examinations and certificates because it allows us to separate the legitimate professionals from the "quacks." The diploma in the doctor's office tells me that the one who offers medical advice has been through a standard program and has been examined.

Is there an examination to distinguish legitimate servants of Christ from those whose claims are insupportable? Second Corinthians has been devoted to that question. The Corinthian church, like any congregation of the Lord's church today, was forced to choose between two opposite types of servants. On the one hand, there was Paul, the founder of this church. He had impressed no one with his showmanship, oratorical skills, or signs of personal power. On the other side were the missionaries who had come to Corinth with great claims of spiritual experiences and power. No accrediting board could certify the genuine ministers and disqualify the "quacks." The Corinthian church was itself the certifying board. Its task was to examine two very different kinds of ministers.

The church is always in the difficult position faced by the Corinthians. We are faced with the conflicting claims of different views of what it means to be a Christian. Therefore, the church has the difficult task of examining which ministries are valid.

An important word lies at the center of the discussion word *dokimazo* means "examine," "test," or "prove" (cf. 13:5). The word was used especially for the testing of precious metals through fire. The fire separated the genuine from the nongenuine elements. The word was also used for the testing of nongenuine elements. The word was also used for the testing of Christians. There is an occasion for Christians to examine their own work (Galatians 6:4). At the Lord's Supper, the Christian "examines himself" (1 Corinthians 11:28). The same word is used for the Christian's responsibility to "test everything" (1 Thessalonians 5:21). In 8:8, Paul encourages the Corinthians to "prove by the earnestness of others that your love also is genuine." Therefore, the Christian is also examined to determine his authenticity.

In the New Testament, the test results either in the disciple's being proven "genuine" (*dokimos*) or false (*adokimos*). Paul frequently describes some Christians as "genuine" (i.e., "having passed the test"). In 1 Corinthians 11:9, he says that the factions in Corinth will result in the recognition of "those who are genuine." In Romans 16:10, he says, "Greet Apollos, who is approved [*dokimos*] in Christ." Apollos had, in some way, "passed the test." As these passages indicate, standards existed by which they could distinguish the genuine (*dokimos*) servant of Christ from the one who fails the test (*adokimos*). In 1 Corinthians 9:27, Paul is concerned lest he be "disqualified" (*adokimos*).

A church that is confronted with many kinds of ministries should recognize that they are not all equally valid. Our responsibility is to know what test to apply.

"SINCE YOU DESIRE PROOF THAT CHRIST IS SPEAKING IN ME" (12:14—13:4)

When Paul wrote 2 Corinthians, he had reached a turning point in his relationship to this congregation. As he indicates in 12:14 and 13:1, he is planning a third visit to the Corinthians. We already know from 2:1-4 that the second visit to this church is still a painful memory for him. He could not easily forget the "painful visit" or the terrible wrong that was done to him (7:12). Nor could he easily forget the many other instances where the Corinthians had caused him emotional torment (cf. 2:13). Now he is prepared to make a third visit, and he writes with considerable anxiety in facing the Corinthians. He desperately wants to avoid another humiliating visit with them (12:21).

In anticipating his third visit to the Corinthians, Paul recognizes that he is on trial. Although he founded and nurtured this church, they have the audacity to demand proof (*dokime*) that Christ speaks through him (13:3). Having criticized Paul for his lack of eloquence (10:10), they observed the extraordinary difference between Paul and the other missionaries. Some demonstration of power in his speaking would certainly make Paul a more credible missionary. If only he would prove that he is speaking for Christ! He says, probably with a touch of irony, in 13:6, "I hope you will find out that we have not failed [*adokimos*]," literally, "that we have not failed the test." The Corinthians have heard the claims of two kinds of ministries. Now they demand that Paul submit his credentials to them!

There was another reason that Paul was challenged to give proof that Christ was speaking in him. Persistent questions were asked about his integrity. Some had charged that Paul was "crafty" and that he took advantage of the church through guile (12:16, 17; cf. 7:2). Paul was not challenged on doctrinal issues alone. He was examined closely for signs of greed and hucksterism (cf. 2:17). Especially where the leader is in the position of encouraging others to give financial support, his integrity may be under suspicion.

How do we supply "proof" to those who demand to see our credentials as servants of Christ? Every Christian leader is, in a sense, confronted with the challenge that is given to Paul in 13:3. It is not enough to offer carefully reasoned arguments for our discipleship. Even the most dedicated Christian servant is challenged to offer proof of his discipleship.

Paul recognizes that he will be under careful observation on his next visit to Corinth. Despite his constant attempt to prevent anyone from finding fault with his ministry (2 Corinthians 6:3; 8:20), there were the lingering doubts about Paul's integrity. Although he never accepted money from the Corinthians, there was the suspicion that he was "crafty," and that he acted with "guile" (12:16). Even the precautions which Paul had taken in sending trusted men like Titus and the other brother (cf. 8:16-18) had not removed the suspicions about Paul's integrity. There was the suspicion that even his elaborate precautions in handling money (cf. chapter 9) were nothing more than a cover for some attempt to take advantage of the people. Not even a shared history, over a period of years, could remove the doubts about Paul, for he lived in an age where traveling missionaries were always greeted with suspicion. The many false apostles had raised the suspicion that, behind the pious claims of every preacher, there was a desire to exploit others.

One way to react to such accusations is to deny them. The "big lie" is one of the oldest tactics to keep a good person on the defensive. When one is "given something to deny," he can hardly be an effective advocate of his cause. Paul appears in 2 Corinthians to have much to deny. "We have taken advantage of no one" (7:2), he claims. He denies that he has been acting with "cunning" or has been tampering with God's Word (2:16). There is a time for denying an unjust charge against our work in order to overcome the suspicions of others.

Denials are never sufficient for "passing the test," for our behavior is the ultimate test of our sincerity. We have noticed already that Paul's major defense of his ministry has been to invite his readers to look at the record and see if his is the record of a huckster (cf. 1:12—2:4). At this crucial moment when Paul is preparing his third visit, he knows that his behavior will be under close examination. Already, according to 12:14-18, he is conscious of his reputation. "I will not be a burden," he says (12:14). It is significant that right before this he has recalled his past history with this church, saying that he did not burden them (12:13). Although he had no objection to receiving financial support from churches (cf. 11:7, 8; 1 Corinthians 9:6-12), he never burdened the Corinthian church (11:9). He preferred to work with his hands as a skilled craftsman (cf. 1 Corinthians 4:12; Acts 18:3) than to accept money from the Corinthian church. Apparently, he preferred, at times, to be in want than to take their money.

On the surface, it seems inconsistent for Paul to be determined not to take money from the Corinthians at the very time that he is supported by the Macedonians (11:8, 9). The apparent inconsistency speaks of Paul's sensitivity about his reputation in money matters. Wherever the slightest suspicion about his integrity existed, he refused to accept money. He would never give any impression that he was enriching himself.

Paul wanted to be remembered as a "man for others." Thus, it was important on this third visit, as on the two previous visits, to demonstrate that he cared more for others than himself. He says, "I seek not what is yours, but you" (12:14). He was interested neither in building his reputation nor in enriching himself. Like an anxious parent (12:14), he had a selfless interest in watching his children mature. Paul's earlier actions had always been dictated by the needs of his churches. He did not intend to change on his third visit.

The extent of Paul's selflessness is remarkable: "I will most gladly spend and be spent for your souls" (12:15). The NEB renders the words, "I will gladly spend what I have for you—yes, and spend myself to the limit." The words could be rendered, "I am ready to sacrifice my own life for you." There are no lengths to which Paul will not go for their salvation. Indeed, according to 13:7, Paul would prefer to "fail" the test (*adokimos*) himself than to have the Corinthians do wrong. His own fate—his health, comfort, and even his life—were not as important as their salvation. He is gladly weak for the sake of making the Corinthians strong (13:9). What matters far more than his reputation, therefore, is their upbuilding, not the winning of an argument (12:19).

Ironically, the "test" of the genuine Christian is that something is more important to him than "passing the test" (13:7). His life has been so determined by service to others that their welfare is more important than his own. Throughout 2 Corinthians, Paul does not often refer to the importance of love; nevertheless, love is the proof of his discipleship. He says, "If I love you the more, am I to be loved the less?" (12:15). Love had led him to make painful visits to the Corinthians (2:1-4). It had motivated him to face humiliation and defeat (11:23-33) without surrendering. When he was criticized for not accepting financial support, he replied, "And why? Because I do not love you? God knows I do" (11:11). Paul lived his Christian life in a "new world" (5:17) where "the love of Christ controls us" (5:14).

The "proof" of Paul's ministry is his love, a love that identifies with the weakness of Jesus at the cross (13:4) and exhausts itself for others. This proof may not be the kind that others had been looking for (13:3), but it was the only kind Paul was willing to give. He had exhausted himself before for a troublesome church. On his third visit, he was willing to do so again.

We live in an age that has heard so much about mail-order churches and Christian leaders who are primarily interested in publicity and power that people have grown cynical. Therefore, we, like Paul, face the demand that we pass the test. We will fail if we have only greater budgets and statistical measurements to offer as proof of our genuineness. We fail also if we take pride, primarily, in our greater place in the community. We only add to the general cynicism when we measure ourselves merely with statistical standards. Likewise, while it is important to provide convenient resources for ourselves, the real test of our ministry is in our reaching to others, not in our turning in on ourselves. The real test is our record in concrete deeds of service.

This theme has been the thread running through 2 Corinthians. We cannot overlook a definite repetition that appears to run through the book. The many references to Paul's own struggles (1:3-11; 2:1-4; 4:7-16; 6:1-10; 11:23-33) are his way of showing us that he cares. His record of anxiety for the churches, bitter disputes with Christians, and persecution and exhaustion are evidence that his ministry is genuine.

Doctrinal correctness is not a substitute for sacrificial love as the test of our service. We might have more restful nights if we kept ourselves detached from the problems of the local church. A professional detachment from its problems would undoubtedly offer us more free time to pursue our own interests and develop our potential. But the test of being a Christian is the capacity to say, "The love of Christ controls us."

"EXAMINE YOURSELVES" (13:5)

Paul is not the only one on trial. His coming visit to the Corinthians will also be a test for them. Those who demanded proof that Christ was speaking in Paul are now told, "Examine yourselves, to see whether you are holding to your faith." (13:5). Paul makes grave warnings. On his third visit, he will use his authority "for building up and not for tearing down" (13:10). On this occasion, he will not spare the disobedient Christians (13:2). It is as if he will be holding trial, and his three visits will themselves be the "witnesses" required for a court hearing (13:1). Those who were giving the test are now being tried. It is time for them to recognize that they must do more than stand in judgment on others. They must test themselves before Paul's visit.

Every ministry has a time for self-examination. We often imply that we can escape the examinations of our own work by directing the focus toward other ministries. We are more comfortable, as the Corinthians were, in challenging others to offer "proof" of their genuine discipleship. But we cannot remain in the role of the examining board. Paul's advice in 13:5 is a reminder that the whole church can cease to be "in the faith." The whole congregation may "fail to meet the test." Paul's challenge, "examine yourself," is a special word to every Christian who prefers the role of examining the credentials of others. Like the Corinthians, we may discover that we have worked with false standards of success and power and that we have developed a lifestyle that does not fit the original proclamation.

What is the test for the church that determines whether it has "passed the test"? We might mention several possible tests, but Paul mentions two in particular. First, he fears that he will find on his third visit characteristics in the Corinthian church which have been a persistent problem with them. He fears that he will find the same quarreling and selfishness that has always been a problem there (12:20; cf. 1 Corinthians 1:11; 4:6). He also fears that he will find the same sexual offenses which had been their problem from the beginning (12:21; 1 Corinthians 5:1; 6:12). One test for the church, therefore, is its changed life. A congregation which has not overcome the selfishness and the lax sexual standards of its culture has not "passed the test," for in Christ there is "a whole new world."

A second test for the Corinthians is this: What kind of identity do these Corinthians want as a congregation? What kinds of ministers and leaders will they listen to? Whether or not the Corinthians "pass the test" depends on whom they acknowledge as having passed their test! Will they acknowledge that the test in every ministry is its relationship to the One who "was crucified in weakness, but lives by the power of God" (13:4)? And will they acknowledge that the true leader is "weak in him," but depends on God's power to survive (13:4)? The purpose of 2 Corinthians can easily be summed up by Paul's challenge in 13:5. A church that looks for direction is being tested by the presence of the many options and programs which look and offer a confusing number of ministries.

CONCLUSION

The temptation of the Corinthians was in choosing ministries which exhibit power, prestige, and influence. According to Paul, a "true Christian" operates with a new set of standards, a "whole new world." Authentic ministry is recognized for its willingness to exhaust itself for others. Our story began with the One who poured Himself out for others at the cross. Consequently, an authentic disciple is one who shares the desire for service to others.